MARIA IRENE FORNES

MARIA IRENE FORNES

PLAYS

**Mud
The Danube
The Conduct of Life
Sarita**

Preface by Susan Sontag

PAJ Publications
(a division of Performing Arts Journal, Inc.)
New York City

Published by PAJ Publications
P.O. Box 260, Village Station
NY, NY 10014

Library of Congress Cataloging in Publication Data
Maria Irene Fornes: Plays
Library of Congress Catalog Card No.: 85-60187
ISBN: 0-933826-83-4 (paper)

Graphic Design: Gautam Dasgupta

Publication of this book has been made possible in part by grants from the National Endowment for the Arts, Washington, D.C., a federal agency, and the New York State Council on the Arts.

General Editors of PAJ Playscripts:
  Bonnie Marranca and Gautam Dasgupta

05 04 03   7 6 5

Contents

Preface

Susan Sontag

Mud, The Danube, The Conduct of Life, Sarita—four plays, recent work by the prolific Maria Irene Fornes, who for many years has been conducting with exemplary tenacity and scrupulousness a unique career in the American theatre.

Born in Havana, Fornes arrived in this country with her family when she was fifteen; in her twenties she spent several years in France (she was painting then), and began writing plays after she returned to New York, when she was around thirty. Although the language in which she became a writer was English, not Spanish—and Fornes's early work is inconceivable without the reinforcement of the lively local New York milieu (particularly the Judson Poets Theatre) in which she surfaced in the early 1960s—she is unmistakably a writer of bicultural inspiration: one very American way of being a writer. Her imagination seems to me to have, among other sources, a profoundly Cuban one. I am reminded of the witty, sensual phantasmagorias of Cuban writers such as Lydia Cabrera, Calvert Casey, Virgilio Piñera.

Of course, writers, these or any other, were not the conscious influences on Fornes or any of the best "downtown" theatre of the 1960s. Art Nouveau and Hollywood Deco had more to do with, say, The Theatre of the Ridiculous, than any plausible literary antecedents (Tzara, Firbank, etc.). This is also true of Fornes, an autodidact whose principal influences were neither theatre nor literature but certain styles of painting and the movies. But unlike similarly influenced New York dramatists, her work did not eventually become parasitic on literature (or opera, or movies). It was never a revolt against theatre, or a theatre recycling fantasies encoded in other genres.

Her two earliest plays prefigure the dual register, one völkisch, the other placeless-international, of all the subsequent work. *The Widow*, a poignant chronicle of a simple life, is set in Cuba, while *Tango Palace*, with its volleys of sophisticated exchanges, takes place in a purely theatrical space: a cave, an altar. Fornes has a complex relation to the strategy of naivete. She is chary of the folkloristic, rightly so. But she is strongly drawn to the pre-literary: to the authority of documents, of found materials such as letters of her great-grandfather's cousin which inspired *The Widow*, the diary of a domestic servant in turn-of-the-century New Hampshire which was transformed into *Evelyn Brown*, Emma's lecture in *Fefu and Her Friends*.

For a while she favored the musical play—in a style reminiscent of the populist parables in musical-*commedia* form preserved in films from the 1930s like René Clair's *A Nous la Liberté*. It was a genre that proclaimed its innocence, and specialized in rueful gaiety. Sharing with the main tradition of modernist drama an aversion to the reductively psychological and to sociological explanations, Fornes chose a theatre of types (such personages as the defective sage and the woman enslaved by sexual dependence reappear in a number of plays) and a theatre of miracles: the talking mirror in *The Office*, the fatal gun wound at the end of *Fefu and Her Friends*. Lately, Fornes seems to be eschewing this effect: the quotidian as something to be violated—by lyricism, by disaster. Characters can still break into song, as they did in the dazzling bittersweet plays of the mid-1960s, like *Promenade* and *Molly's Dream* and *The Successful Life of 3*. But the plays are less insistently charming. Reality is less capricious. More genuinely lethal—as in *Eyes on the Harem*, *Sarita*.

Character is revealed through catechism. People requiring or giving instruction is a standard situation in Fornes's plays. The desire to be initiated, to be taught, is depicted as an essential, and essentially pathetic, longing. (Fornes's elaborate sympathy for the labor of thought is the endearing observation of someone who is almost entirely self-taught.) And there are many dispensers of wisdom in Fornes's plays, apart from those—*Tango Palace*, *Doctor Kheal*—specifically devoted to the comedy and the pathos of instruction. But Fornes is neither literary nor anti-literary. These are not cerebral exercises or puzzles but the real questions, about . . . the conduct of life. There is much wit but no nonsense. No banalities. And no non sequiturs.

While some plays are set in never-never land, some have local flavors —like the American 1930s of *Fefu and Her Friends*. Evoking a specific setting, especially when it is Hispanic (this being understood as an underprivileged reality), or depicting the lives of the oppressed and humiliated, especially when the subject is that emblem of oppression, the woman servant, such plays as *Evelyn Brown* and *The Conduct of Life* may seem more "realistic"—given the condescending assumptions of the ideology of realism. (Oppressed women, particularly domestic servants and prostitutes, have long been the signature subject of what is sometimes called realism, sometimes naturalism.) But I am not convinced that Fornes's recent work is any less a theatre of fantasy than it was, or more now a species of dramatic realism. Her work is both a theatre about utterance (i.e., a meta-theatre) and a theatre about the disfavored—both Handke *and* Kroetz, as it were.

It was always a theatre of heartbreak. But at the beginning the mood was often throwaway, playful. Now it's darker, more passionate: consider the twenty-year trajectory that goes from *The Successful Life of 3* to *Mud*, about the unsuccessful life of three. She writes increasingly from a woman's point of view. Women are doing women's things—performing unrewarded labor (in *Evelyn Brown*), getting raped (in *The Conduct of Life*)—and also, as in *Fefu and Her Friends*, incarnating the human condition as such. Fornes has a near faultless ear for the ruses of egotism and cruelty. Unlike most contemporary dramatists, for whom psychological brutality is the principal, inexhaustible subject, Fornes is never in complicity with the brutality she depicts. She has an increasingly expressive relation to dread, to grief and to passion—in *Sarita*, for example, which is about sexual passion and the incompatibilities of desire. Dread is not just a subjective state but is attached to history: the psychology of torturers (*The Conduct of Life*), nuclear war (*The Danube*).

Fornes's work has always been intelligent, often funny, never vulgar or cynical; both delicate and visceral. Now it is something more. (The turning point, I think, was the splendid *Fefu and Her Friends*—with its much larger palette of sympathies, for both Julia's incurable despair and Emma's irrepressible jubilation.) The plays have always been about wisdom: what it means to be wise. They are getting wiser.

It is perhaps not appropriate here to do more than allude to her great distinction and subtlety as a director of her own plays, and as an inspiring and original teacher (working mainly with young Hispanic-American playwrights). But it seems impossible not to connect the truthfulness in Fornes's plays, their alertness of depicting, their unfacile compassionateness, with a certain character, a certain virtue. In the words of a Northern Sung landscape painter, Kuo Hsi, if the artist "can develop a natural, sincere, gentle, and honest heart, then he will immediately be able to comprehend the aspect of tears and smiles and of objects, pointed or oblique, bent or inclined, and they will be so clear in his mind that he will be able to put them down spontaneously with his paint brush."

Hers seems to be an admirable temperament, unaffectedly independent, highminded, ardent. And one of the few agreeable spectacles which our culture affords is to watch the steady ripening of this beautiful talent.

MARIA IRENE FORNES

PLAYS

Mud

a play in 17 scenes

The first draft of *Mud* was created and performed at the 6th Padua Hills Festival, Claremont, California, in July, 1983. It was directed and designed by the author, with the following cast:

Lloyd	Gregory Pace
Mae	Mary Jo Pearson
Henry	John O'Keefe

The present version was presented at the Theater for the New City, 162 2nd Avenue, New York City, on November 10, 1983. It was directed by the author.

CHARACTERS:

Mae: A spirited young woman. She is single-minded and determined, a believer. She is mid-twenties.

Lloyd: A simple and good-hearted young man. He is ungainly and unkempt. His shoulders slope, his stomach protrudes, some of his teeth are missing. At the start of the play, illness contributes to his poor appearance. He is mid-twenties.

Henry: A large man. He has a natural sense of dignity, a philosophical mind. He can barely read. He is mid-fifties.

The set is a wooden room which sits on an earth promontory. The promontory is five feet high and covers the same periphery as the room. The wood has the color and texture of bone that has dried in the sun. It is ashen and cold. The earth in the promontory is red and soft and so is the earth around it. There is no greenery. Behind the promontory there is a vast blue sky. On the back wall of the room there is an oversized fireplace which is the same color and texture as the walls and floor. On each side of the fireplace there are narrow doors. The door to the right leads to the exterior. There is a blue sky. The one to the left leads to a dark corridor. In the center of the room there is a kitchen table. There is a chair on each end. Down right there is an ironing board. There is an iron on it and a pair of trousers. Against the back wall on the left there is another chair. After the first scene these three chairs will always be placed around the table and will be referred to as right, center, and left. Against the right wall there is a bench. On it there is a pile of unpressed trousers. On the table there is a pile of pressed trousers. Under the bench, there is a bundle of women's clothes and a pair of old, flat women's shoes. Inside the fireplace there are two cardboard boxes. One is full and tied with a string, the other is empty. On the mantelpiece there are, from right to left: a brown paper bag with a pamphlet in it, a pot with three metal plates and three spoons stacked upon it, a plate with broken bread, a pitcher with milk, a textbook, a notebook and pencil, a dish with string beans, a folded newspaper and a box with pills. Between the fireplace and the door to the left there are an ax and a rifle.

Offstage there is an empty box the same size as the box tied with a string. The following props are carried by the actors as they enter to perform the scene:

Mae: 2 bundles of clothes and a loose clean rag.

Lloyd: 3 coins, a prescription note and a cup with oatmeal and a spoon.

Henry: lipstick wrapped in paper, a small mirror, a notebook, bills and pencil, loose coins, a tin cup of milk, and a wad of bills.

At the end of each scene a freeze is indicated. These freezes will last eight seconds which will create the effect of a still photograph. When the freeze is broken, the actors will make the necessary set changes and proceed to perform the following scene.

ACT ONE

Scene 1

Lloyd sits left. He is unwashed and unshaven. He has a fever. He is clumsy and badly coordinated. Mae is at the ironing board. She is unkempt.

LLOYD: You think you learn a lot at school?
MAE: I do.
LLOYD: What do you learn?
MAE: Subjects.
LLOYD: What is subjects?
MAE: Different things.
LLOYD: What things?
MAE: You want to know?
LLOYD: What are they?
MAE: Arithmetic.
LLOYD: Big deal arithmetic. I know arithmetic.
MAE: I'll bet.
LLOYD: Don't talk back to me. I'll kick your ass.
MAE: Fuck you, Lloyd. I'm telling you about arithmetic and you talk to me like that? You're a moron. I won't tell you anything.
LLOYD: Oh, no?
MAE: No.
LLOYD: So what's arithmetic?
MAE: Fuck you. I'm not telling you.
LLOYD: (*Moving toward her.* I'll fuck you till you're blue in the face! (*He stops and starts back to the chair.*) I don't even want to fuck you.
MAE: You can't, that's why. You can't get it up.
LLOYD: Oh yeah? I got it up yesterday!
MAE: When!
LLOYD: Afternoon!

MAE: Never saw it.

LLOYD: You weren't here.

MAE: Where was I?

LLOYD: At school. You missed it. I got it up.

MAE: Who with?

LLOYD: Fuck you. I'm not telling you.

MAE: Who with?

LLOYD: With myself.—I don't need someone. I got it up right here. (*Pointing to the wall.*) See that? I did that! From here. I didn't give it to you or anyone. (*Pantomiming an erection and ejaculation.*) I held it as long as I wanted. Then I gave it to the wall. (*Pointing to a spot on the wall.*) See. Fuck you, Mae.

MAE: Fuck you, Lloyd.

LLOYD: So tell me!

MAE: Tell you what.

LLOYD: What's arithmetic?

MAE: It's numbers.

LLOYD: Oh yeah!

MAE: Yeah!

LLOYD: Why didn't you say it's numbers!—I know numbers.

MAE: You don't know numbers.

LLOYD: Yes I do. (*He stands.*) I'm Lloyd. I have two pigs. My mother died. I was seven. My father left. He is dead. (*He gets three coins from his pocket.*) This is money. It's mine. It's three nickels. I'm Lloyd. That's arithmetic.

MAE: That is not arithmetic.

LLOYD: Why not?

MAE: It isn't.

LLOYD: (*He returns to the chair.*) It's numbers!

MAE: Arithmetic is more!

LLOYD: What more!

MAE: A lot more!—Multiplication!

LLOYD: Come here! (*She puts the iron down.*)

MAE: What for!

LLOYD: I'm going to show you something.

MAE: (*She walks to him.*) What!

LLOYD: (*In one move he takes her hand, crosses his left leg, and puts her hand on his crotch.*) Feel it!

MAE: What?

LLOYD: It! It! Touch it!

MAE: I'm touching it!

LLOYD: Do something to it!

MAE: What!

LLOYD: Anything, stupid!

MAE: Let go of my hand!

LLOYD: (*Pressing her tighter.*) What hand?

MAE: Let go, you jerk! You stink! You smell bad!

LLOYD: So what!

MAE: You're disgusting!

LLOYD: No kidding!

MAE: Let go! (*She steps on his foot.*)

LLOYD: Shit! (*She goes back to the ironing board.*) I'll kick your ass! (*He feels his genitals.*) Shit, it's gone!

MAE: What's gone! You can't get it up! You have some sickness there! (*Short pause.*) You should go to a doctor.

LLOYD: Didn't I say I got it up yesterday!

MAE: Yes. You did.

LLOYD: OK! So I did!—So where's dinner!

MAE: I don't know where's dinner.

LLOYD: You know where's dinner!

MAE: You know where's dinner!

LLOYD: Yeah, where's dinner! Dinner's in a pot on the stove! Dinner's on the table! It's in the cupboard! It's dried up in the pot! Dinner is somewhere! It's spilled on the floor! Where's dinner! (*There is a pause.*) *Where's dinner!* (*She continues ironing.*) Come here!

MAE: Fuck you.

LLOYD: You're a whore!

MAE: I'm pressing, jerk! What are you doing! I'm pressing. What are you doing! (*He looks away.*) I'm pressing what are you doing! You're a jerk. (*She continues ironing.*) I work. See, I work. I'm working. I learned to work. I wake up and I work. Open my eyes and I work. I work. What do you do! Yeah, what do you do!—*Work!*

LLOYD: So what. (*He sits in a corner on the floor.*)

MAE: What do you do when you open your eyes. I work, jerk. You're a pig. You'll die like a pig in the mud. You'll rot there in the mud. No one will bury you. Your skin will bloat. In the mud. Then, it will get blue like rotten meat and it will bloat even more. And you will get so rotten that the dogs will puke when they come near you. Even flies won't go near you. You'll just lay there and rot. (*She irons.*) I'm going to die in a hospital. In white sheets. You hear? (*She looks front.*) Clean feet. Injections. That's how I'm going to die. I'm going to die clean. I'm going to school and I'm learning things. You're stupid. I'm not. When I finish school I'm leaving. You hear that? You can stay in the mud. (*She irons.*) Did you pick the corn?

LLOYD: What corn?

MAE: The corn I told you to pick.

LLOYD: There is no corn.

MAE: How come there is no corn.

LLOYD: The groundhog ate it.

MAE: You let him eat it.

LLOYD: I didn't.

MAE: You didn't watch it.

LLOYD: I came in to sleep. I had to sleep.

MAE: You can sleep in the field.

LLOYD: It's wet there! It's cold! I'm sick! You sleep there!

MAE: I work here, not in the field.

LLOYD: I'll work here. You work there.

MAE: (*Harshly.*) I wish you went to the doctor.—You're not going to get well if you don't. When I leave you'll starve.

LLOYD: I'll find food.

MAE: Where?

LLOYD: Anywhere. There's food.

MAE: Where.

LLOYD: There's pigslop.

MAE: What pigslop? There won't be any pigslop. Not if you don't grow something to put in it!

(*Pause.*)

LLOYD: I did it to Betsy.

MAE: You did.

LLOYD: Yeah.—I felt bad.—My head hurt.—I went to her. She's nice. She lets me eat her food.—I did it to her.—I got it up. I got it in her all the way.—It didn't hurt.

MAE: No kidding.

LLOYD: It didn't hurt.

MAE: You don't fuck pigs.

LLOYD: She liked it.

MAE: I'll bet.

LLOYD: What do you mean?

MAE: Did you get clean before you did it?

LLOYD: What for? I'm clean.

MAE: No you're not. You stink.

LLOYD: She didn't mind.

MAE: (*She places the ironing board alongside the right wall and places the garment she has pressed on top of the other pressed clothes.*) I'm taking these up now. We'll walk to the clinic. You have to see a doctor. (*She starts putting on her shoes.*) Put on your shoes, Lloyd.—I'll walk there with you. I know you won't get there if I don't go with you. Get moving, Lloyd. (*She takes the clothes and goes to the door.*) Come on. (*He doesn't move.*) Let's go, Lloyd. (*He stands and goes for the ax. He holds the ax as he waits for her to exit.*) You're not going to the clinic with an ax.

LLOYD: (*He goes to the chair still holding the ax and sits.*) Why not.

MAE: You can't.

LLOYD: I'll take my knife, then.

MAE: You can't take your knife either.

LLOYD: I won't go then.

(*They freeze.*)

Scene 2

Mae takes a brown paper bag from the mantelpiece, opens the right door, steps on the threshold and turns front as if she had just come from the outside. She has an air of serenity. Lloyd sits on the left. His appearance has worsened.

MAE: I went to the clinic, Lloyd. And I told them what you have.

LLOYD: What did you tell them?

MAE: (*Stepping into the room.*) I told them you're sick. And I told them what you have.

LLOYD: What did they say?

MAE: They said you have to go there. (*As she gets the chair from the left corner and places it center.*) You have to go to the clinic. They won't give you medicine till you go.

LLOYD: I'm not going.

MAE: They have to give you a test. They can't give you medicine till they find out what you have. They said you may have something bad.

LLOYD: What.

MAE: (*She sits.*) They didn't say. (*She takes a pamphlet out of the paper bag.*) They gave me this book.

LLOYD: What does it say?

MAE: (*She places the paper bag on the mantelpiece.*) I couldn't read it. I tried to read it but I can't. I got Henry to read it for you. He's outside.

LLOYD: Why can't you read it?

MAE: It's too difficult.

LLOYD: All that time at school and you can't read.

MAE: I tried to read it and it was too difficult. That's why I got Henry to read it because it was too difficult for me. It is advanced. I'm not advanced yet. I'm intermediate. I can read a lot of things but not this.—I'm going to let Henry in.

LLOYD: (*Reproachfully.*) I wish you could have read it.

MAE: Me too. I wish I could have read it. (*She opens the door and walks to the left of the center chair.*) Come in, Henry. (*Henry enters and stands by the fireplace. He places his left hand on the mantelpiece.*) Sit down, Henry. (*Henry sits on the center chair. Mae closes the door.*) Here's Henry, Lloyd. He's going to read for you.

HENRY: Are you drunk, Lloyd? You look drunk.

MAE: (*Sitting on the right.*) He's sick. He has a fever.

HENRY: Has he been drinking?

LLOYD: I am not drunk.

HENRY: What's wrong with him?

MAE: He's sick.

HENRY: Remember Ron, what happened to him.

LLOYD: What happened to him?

HENRY: He died.—And what did he die of?

LLOYD: He drank till he died.

MAE: His liver failed him.

HENRY: Why did his liver fail him? Alcohol.—Why did he drink? He drank because he owned alcohol. And why did he own alcohol? He owned alcohol because he owned a pharmacy. And why did that lead a man to drinking? Because he kept alcohol in the pharmacy.—There you have two things: alcohol and time to do nothing. So what happens? You drink yourself to death.—So, you have alcohol, you drink it. You don't have alcohol, you don't drink it. You have money to buy alcohol, you buy it. You don't have money to buy it, you don't buy it.—Does Lloyd have alcohol, Mae?

MAE: He has no money to buy it.

HENRY: If Lloyd had money he would drink. He'd be a drunk.

MAE: Yes, he would.

HENRY: If he's not a drunk it's because he's poor.

MAE: He is.—This is the book, Henry.

HENRY: (*Henry puts on his glasses. He reads each section first to himself in a low voice. Then he reads it out loud stumbling through the words at a high speed.*) Prostatitis and Prostatosis. Acute and chronic bacterial infection of the prostrate gland: symptoms, diagnosis, and treatment. (*He wets his finger and turns the page.*) Common symptoms of acute prostatitis and bacterial prostatosis are: febrile illness, back pains, perineal pain, irritative voiding, aching of the perineum, sexual pain, sexual impotency, painful ejaculation, and intermittent disureah, or bloody ejaculation.

LLOYD: What does that mean?

HENRY: I don't know what it means, Lloyd. These are medical terms. It needs study. This may require the use of a dictionary—a special dictionary. One that has medical terms—technical terms—probably a dictionary that would have all kinds of technical terms—from hardware and construction terms to scientific terms—like physics. There are such dictionaries. (*Short pause.*) You look swollen, Lloyd.

MAE: He is swollen.

HENRY: And your color is poor.

MAE: Show him your tongue, Lloyd. His tongue is white and his breath smells bad.

(*Lloyd opens his mouth. Henry looks at Lloyd's tongue.*)

HENRY: What is wrong with you?

MAE: I want him to go to the doctor but he won't.

HENRY: Why won't you go to the doctor, Lloyd.

LLOYD: I don't want to go.

MAE: He will stay here and rot.

LLOYD: I won't rot. I said I'd go. You said I couldn't go.

MAE: He wanted to go up with an ax. He's an animal. You don't go to the clinic with an ax. You can't do that.

HENRY: Why would you do that, Lloyd?

LLOYD: I didn't do it. I never went.

HENRY: He does smell bad.

MAE: He's rotting away and he won't do anything about it. You better dig your grave while you can, Lloyd. Because I'm not going to do it for you. I told him to find a spot and dig it. It takes a strong person to dig that deep. I can't do it. I wouldn't, even if I could. (*Pause.*) Would you like some bread, Henry? I got some butter.

HENRY: Yes, thank you.

MAE: Would you like some dinner? We have soup.

HENRY: Yes, thank you.

MAE: Stay then, I haven't started it yet.

HENRY: I will, thank you.

(*They freeze.*)

Scene 3

Mae places the pamphlet on the mantelpiece, then takes the pot, plates and spoons and places them on the table. They each take a spoon and plate, then they pass them to Mae, who holds the plates in her hands as if she were about to put them away. Lloyd lies on the floor, under the table, facing front. Henry moves his chair slightly to the left. He and Mae have been talking. They both speak with philosophical objectivity.

HENRY: Soon everything will be used only once. We will use things once. We will need to do that as our time will be of value and it will not be feasible to spend it caring for things: washing them, mending them, repairing them. We will use a car till it breaks down. Then, we will discard it. A radio or any machine or appliance will be discarded as soon as it breaks down. We will make a call on the telephone and a new one will be delivered. Already we see places that use paper cups, paper plates, paper towels.—Our time will not be wasted and we will choose how to spend it.

MAE: I don't think I'll be wanted in such a world.

HENRY: Why not?

MAE: . . . Oh. (*Pause.*) In such a world a person must be of value.

HENRY: Oh?

MAE: I feel I am hollow . . . and offensive. (*As Mae places the dishes on the mantelpiece.*)

HENRY: Why is that?

MAE: I think most people are.

HENRY: What do you mean?—Explain what you mean.

MAE: I don't think I can.

HENRY: I am not offensive. I don't think I am offensive. I think I am a decent man.

MAE: You are decent, Henry. I know you are, and so is Lloyd in his own way.

HENRY: Then, what do you mean when you say we are offensive?

MAE: I mean that we are base, and that we spend our lives with small things.

HENRY: I don't feel I do that.

MAE: Don't be offended, Henry. You are not base. Of all the people I know you are the finest. You are the person I respect and I feel most proud to know.—(*She begins to look at him fixedly, possessed by fervor.*) I have no one to talk to. And sometimes I feel hollow and base. And I feel I don't have a mind. But when I talk to you I do. I feel I have a mind. Why is that? (*She moves closer to him.*) Why is it that some people make you feel stupid and some people make you feel smart. Not smart, because I am not smart. But some people make you feel that you have something inside you. Inside your head. (*She moves closer.*) Why is it that you can talk, Henry, and Lloyd cannot talk? Why is that? What I'm saying, Henry, is that I want you. That I want you here with me. That I love you.

HENRY: Mae, this is unexpected.

MAE: It is unexpected, Henry.

HENRY: I have nothing to offer you.

MAE: Yes, you do. I want you.

HENRY: Me?

MAE: (*She starts to move her head toward him slowly and intensely.*) I want your mind.

HENRY: . . . My mind?

MAE: (*Still moving her head toward him.*) I want it. (*She kisses him intensely. They look at each other.*)

HENRY: Did you feel my mind?

MAE: Yes. I did. (*She kisses him again.*) I did. I want you here.

HENRY: Here?

MAE: I want you here.

HENRY: To live here?

MAE: If you will.

(*They freeze.*)

Scene 4

Henry exits. Mae places the spoons and pot on the mantelpiece. Then, she takes off her shoes, places a pair of trousers on the ironing board and puts out the ironing board. Lloyd gets the box with the string from the fireplace and stands down left holding it. Mae irons.

MAE: Just put it down. (*He stands still. She continues ironing.*) Put it down Lloyd. (*He stands still.*) Henry is going to stay here with us. He is going to live here. He needs a place and I want him to stay here. You can learn from Henry. If you want to, he can teach you how to read. Put the box down. I'll take it up to the bedroom. Henry's going to sleep in the bedroom. He has a bad back and he needs to sleep in the bed. You can sleep here.—Get papers from the shed and lay them on the floor. I'll get you a blanket.—I'll take it up now. (*She takes the box from Lloyd and exits left. He is distraught. He sits on the chair on the left and cries. He puts his head on the table and freezes.*)

Scene 5

Mae places the ironing board against the wall. Lloyd places the pitcher of milk and the plate with bread on the table. Mae gets the plates and spoons. She places the spoons in the center and lays each plate in front of her. Henry enters and sits center. Lloyd sits left. Lloyd and Henry take a spoon each. Mae serves bread onto the plates, pours milk on the bread and passes two plates to Henry, who passes one to Lloyd and keeps the second for himself. Mae sits. They start eating.

MAE: Do you say grace before a meal, Henry?

HENRY: I do sometimes.

MAE: Would you say grace?

HENRY: I will, if you want me to.

MAE: I do.

HENRY: (*Crosses his hands.*) Oh, give thanks unto the Lord, for he is good: for his mercy endures forever. For he satisfies the longing soul, and fills the hungry soul with goodness.

MAE: We never said grace in this house. My father never did and I never learned how and neither did Lloyd.—Lloyd did you hear that? Henry said grace. I feel grace in my heart. I feel fresh inside as if a breeze had just gone inside my heart. What was it you said, Henry? What were these words. I don't retain the words. I never do. I find it hard to retain words I learn. It is hard for me to do the work at school. I can work on my feet all day at the ironing board. I can make myself do it, even if I am tired. But I cannot make myself retain what I learn. I have no memory. The teacher says I have no memory. And it's true I don't. I don't remember the things I learn too well. Not enough to pass the test. But I rejoice with the knowledge that I get. Not everything, but most things, make me feel joyful. Do you feel that way, Henry?

HENRY: I am not sure. I like to know things. But if I didn't remember what I learned, I don't think I would feel any pleasure.—If I didn't remember things, I would feel that I don't know them. I like to learn things so I can live according to them, according to my knowledge. What would be the use of knowing things if they don't serve you, if they don't help you shape your life.—Lloyd, do you take pleasure in learning if you forget what you have learned?

(*Lloyd looks at Mae, then at Henry again.*)

MAE: Lloyd doesn't like learning things.

LLOYD: I like learning things.

MAE: Why don't you then?

LLOYD: What is it I haven't learned?

(*Mae and Henry look at each other.*)

MAE: Henry, would you say grace again?

HENRY: Again?

MAE: Is that wrong?

HENRY: No. Oh, give thanks unto the Lord, for he is good: for his mercy endures forever. For he satisfies the longing soul, and fills the hungry soul with goodness. (*Mae sobs.*) Why are you crying?

MAE: I am a hungry soul. I am a longing soul. I am an empty soul. (*She cries.*) I cry with joy. It satisfies me to hear words that speak so lovingly to my soul. (*Mae eats. Lloyd eats. Henry watches Mae.*) Don't be afraid to eat from our dishes, Henry. They are clean.

(*They freeze.*)

Scene 6

Lloyd places his plate and spoon over Henry's. Henry places the pitcher and bread plate on the mantelpiece and exits. Mae places the plates and spoons on the mantelpiece and gets the textbook. She sits center and reads with difficulty. She follows the written words with the fingers of both hands. Her reading is inspired. Lloyd listens to her and stares at the book.

MAE: The starfish is an animal, not a fish. He is called a fish because he lives in the water. The starfish cannot live out of the water. If he is moist and in the shade he may be able to live out of the water for a day. Starfish eat old and dead sea animals. They keep the water clean. A starfish has five arms like a star. That is why it is called a starfish. Each of the arms of the starfish has an eye in the end. These eyes do not look like our eyes. A starfish's eye cannot see. But they can tell if it is night or day. If a starfish loses an arm he can grow a new one. This takes about a year. A starfish can live five or ten years or perhaps more, no one really knows.

(*Lloyd slaps the book off the table. Mae slaps Lloyd. They freeze.*)

Scene 7

Lloyd picks up the book and places it on the down-left corner of the table. He places the left chair against the wall and sits. Mae takes a notebook and pencil from the mantelpiece. She takes the book and stands on the up-

right side of the table copying from the book. Henry enters and stands on the up-left corner.

HENRY: What is Lloyd to you? (*There is a pause.*) He's a man and he's not a blood relative. So what is he to you?

MAE: Lloyd? (*Pause.*) He is like family.

HENRY: But he is not.—Everyone knows he is not. What is he?

MAE: I don't know what you call what he is. If I were to ask myself I would not know what to answer.—He is not with me. You know he is not. He sleeps down here.

HENRY: I feel I am offending him. And he is offending me. So what is he.

MAE: (*Sitting on the right facing front.*) What can I do, Henry, I don't want you to be offended. There's nothing I can do and there's nothing you can do and there is nothing Lloyd can do. He's always been here, since he was little. My dad brought him in. He said that Lloyd was a good boy and that he could keep me company. He said he was old and tired and he didn't understand what a young person like me was like. That he had no patience left and he was weary of life and he had no more desire to make things work. He didn't want to listen to me talk and he felt sorry to see me sad and lonely. He didn't want to be mean to me, but he didn't have the patience. He was sick. My dad was good but he was sad and hopeless and when my mom died he went to hell with himself. He got sick and died and he left Lloyd here and Lloyd and I took care of each other. I don't know what we are. We are related but I don't know what to call it. We are not brother and sister. We are like animals who grow up together and mate. We were mates till you came here, but not since then. I could not be his mate again, not while you are here. I am not an animal. I care about things, Henry, I do. I know some things that I never learned. It's just that I don't know what they are. I cannot grasp them. (*She goes on her knees as her left shoulder leans on the corner of the table.*) I don't want to live like a dog. (*Pause.*) Lloyd is good, Henry. And this is his home. (*Pause. She looks up.*) When you came here I thought heaven had come to this place, and I still feel so. How can there be offense here for you?

(*They freeze.*)

Scene 8

Lloyd places his chair by the table and exits. Mae places the notebook, pencil and textbook on the mantelpiece. She places the dish with string beans center and sits. She snaps beans. Henry walks behind Mae and covers her eyes. He takes a small package from his pocket and puts it in the bowl.

MAE: What is it? (*He uncovers her eyes. She unwraps the package. It is a lipstick.*) Lipstick . . . (*Henry pushes the lipstick out of the tube. He takes a mirror out of his pocket and holds it in front of her.*) A mirror. (*She holds the mirror and puts on lipstick. She puckers her lips. He kisses her.*) Oh, Henry.

(*They freeze.*)

Scene 9

Mae places the lipstick, mirror, and dish with string beans on the mantelpiece. She places the textbook center and sits. Henry places the paper and lipstick cover on the mantelpiece. He takes the newspaper, turns the left chair toward the down-left corner and sits to read, leaning his elbow on the table. Lloyd sits on the floor, down of the right chair with his arm leaning on it.

MAE: (*Reading.*) This is a hermit crab. He is called a hermit because he lives in empty shells that once belonged to other animals. When he is little he likes to crawl into the shells of water snails. When he grows larger he finds a larger shell. Often he tries several shells before he finds the one that fits. Sometimes he wants the shell of another hermit crab and then there is a fight. Sometimes the owner is pulled out. Sometimes the owner wins and stays.

(*Lloyd lifts himself up to look at Henry. He mouths a curse. Mae turns to look at Lloyd, then looks at Henry. Henry turns to look at Mae, then he looks at Lloyd. They freeze.*)

ACT TWO

Scene 10

Henry enters left carrying a notebook, pencil and a few bills. He sits left. He transfers figures from the bills to the ledger. Lloyd enters right. He stands up-center. He reaches into his pocket for a medical prescription and stretches his arm in Henry's direction. He sits to the right. The italicized words represent a stuttering.

LLOYD: They gave me *this*.

HENRY: (*Reads what's on the paper while still in Lloyd's hand. He returns to his papers.*) That's the prescription for your medicine.

LLOYD: They said I should buy *this*. (*Pause.*) They said I should *buy* it.

HENRY: Did you?

LLOYD: No.

HENRY: Why not.

LLOYD: I went to the *clinic*.

HENRY: (*Without looking at him.*) I'm glad you did.

LLOYD: It took a *while*. I thought they *kept* me a long time. I went *early* and just came back.

HENRY: How do you feel?

LLOYD: I don't feel *better*.—I feel *worse*.

HENRY: Why is that?

LLOYD: They have *instruments* there. They *stuck instruments* in me.

HENRY: What did they say?

LLOYD: I have to take *medicine—pills*. I have to *buy* them. They said I have to *swallow* the pills.

HENRY: I'm glad you went.

LLOYD: (*Stretches his arm to show Henry the prescription.*) They gave me *this*. They said I should *buy* this. (*He puts the prescription on the table.*) They said I should *buy* it.

HENRY: (*With contained anger.*) You should get the medicine, Lloyd. You should take it and get it over with. You should take the medication and get well. You should not walk around with an illness that's eating your insides. Get the medicine. Do as you are told.

(*They freeze.*)

Scene 11

Henry exits. Lloyd takes the box of pills from the mantelpiece and empties it on the table. He sits center. Mae enters right, wiping her wet hands with her skirt. She sits right. Lloyd puts a pill in his mouth. A moment later he spits it.

MAE: What are they?

LLOYD: Pills.

MAE: Lloyd . . . What are you doing? (*He cleans his tongue.*) Does it taste bad?

LLOYD: Yeah.

MAE: (*She picks up the pill and sits.*) Try it again. (*He puts it in his mouth.*) Swallow it. (*He swallows and chokes. She stands by him and pushes the pill down his throat. She looks at him.*) Did you swallow it? (*She looks at him.*) What do you feel? (*He makes a face. She sits and puts the pills in the box.*) How did you get them?

LLOYD: (*Defensively.*) I bought them.—I took the money.—From Henry.
—From his trousers.—I took the money from his trousers.—I don't care.—He owes me money.—For rent.—For my bed.—He took my bed.—Like a crab.—He got into my bed like a crab.—I took it.—I didn't steal it, because it belonged to me.—Because I needed to get my medicine.—And he never gave me what he owed me.—I had to ask him for it.—And he never gave it to me.—I asked him.—And he never gave it to me.—And he came here only to take things from me.—Like a crab.

(*Henry enters left. He is in his underwear. He carries his pants over his left arm. He holds a change purse in his right hand. He walks down left and stands there. He is stunned.*)

HENRY: Someone took money from my purse.—There is less money here than I should have.—Some of the money I had is gone.

MAE: Lloyd took it.

HENRY: (*He sits.*) Well, tell him to give it back.

MAE: He took it for his medicine.

HENRY: He went to my purse and took it?

MAE: He needed money for his medicine. (*Pause.*) Would you let Lloyd have that money?

HENRY: Have Lloyd have my money?

(*Pause.*)

MAE: He'll pay it back.

HENRY: How will he pay it back?

MAE: (*To Lloyd.*) . . . Lloyd. . .? (*Lloyd looks at Mae.*)

HENRY: How will he pay it back. How will Lloyd get money to pay me back? (*Pause.*) How much money did he take?

MAE: . . . Lloyd. . . ?

LLOYD: I don't know how much I took.

HENRY: How will he pay it back if he doesn't know how much he took? (*Pause.*) Tell him I want to know how much he took.

LLOYD: I went to the clinic.—And they put those instruments in me.—And they said I had to buy that medicine.—And I couldn't find someone to help me buy that medicine.—I went to the pharmacy. —And they said I had to pay for it.—And Henry had money but he wouldn't pay for it.—And he took my bed.—And he can take anything he wants from me.—And I had to buy that medicine.—So I took the money from him.

HENRY: Ask him when he took it.

LLOYD: I took it while he slept.

HENRY: How much did he take?

(*Pause.*)

MAE: Lloyd can't count, Henry.

HENRY: (*He takes money out of the purse, puts it on the table and counts it. He does mental subtraction.*) Tell him he took one fifty four. (*Mae looks at Lloyd.*) Is that what he spent? Does he still have any of that money? (*Lloyd reaches into his pocket.*) Tell him to put it on the table. (*Lloyd does. Henry counts the money, then does mental subtraction. He puts the coins in the purse and goes to the door.*) Tell him he owes me one thirty eight. And tell him I wish he'll pay it back. (*He exits. Mae goes to the door and looks in the direction Henry has walked. They freeze.*)

Scene 12

Mae puts a pair of trousers on the ironing board and puts the ironing board out. Lloyd places the box of pills on the mantelpiece and stands on top of the table.

LLOYD: There is a reason why it happened to him and not to me.

MAE: I wish it had happened to you.

LLOYD: Ha!—It couldn't have happened to me. I'm strong. He's weak and old. That's why he fell. (*Doing an exaggerated demonstration of someone walking on dangerous ground.*) I can walk on wet stones and I don't fall. Look. I can run on wet stones. I can stand on my own two feet. Look! (*He jumps to the floor and stands with his feet apart.*) Try and push me. Go on. Push me. (*She ignores him. He jumps on the table in a prone position with his legs crossed and his hands under his head.*) I wish he had drowned. I wish he had fallen in the water and drowned. He's old. His legs couldn't hold him. That's why he fell. (*He jumps to the floor and runs across jumping up in the air making sounds as he goes up and down. He does this several times, then holds an athletic pose.*) Can he do that?

MAE: (*Still ironing.*) No, he can't. He's paralyzed. He may be a cripple. You know he can't do that!

LLOYD: (*Lies on the table with his hands under his head.*) He couldn't do it before he fell. That's why he fell. He's old. He was falling apart. That's why he fell. Now he can't even move.—Look! (*He does several cartwheels.*) Can he do that?

MAE: No, he can't.

LLOYD: (*Sits on the table with his arms and legs in a body-builder's pose.*) He has no muscle. I wouldn't fall if I had to walk on wet stones. I can run on wet stones. Like this. (*He demonstrates.*) I wish he had fell in the water. I wish he had drowned. So now he can't walk. (*Short pause.*) Who's going to take care of him?

MAE: We are.

(*Lloyd exits right. The sound of vomiting is heard. She freezes.*)

Scene 13

Mae puts the ironing board alongside the wall. Lloyd enters left with the cup with oatmeal and the spoon. He places the right chair away from the table. Henry enters. He sits on the chair to the right. His left side is paralyzed and deformed. His trousers are rolled to his knees. He is bare-

chested and wears a kitchen towel as a bib. He wears a necktie under the towel. He holds a tin cup of milk in his left hand. Lloyd is perched against the table next to Henry. He feeds oatmeal to him. Henry moves the oatmeal around his mouth, then he lets it dribble out or he spits it. Henry's speech is incomprehensible.

LLOYD: Stop it! (*Scooping the spilled oatmeal from Henry's chin and bib and putting it back in his mouth.*) Stop doing that.—Don't do that. (*Henry lets the oatmeal out.*) You just quit that.—Chew it.—Swallow it. (*Henry lets the oatmeal out. Lloyd starts scooping it.*) Stop that! Stop doing that! You better stop that, Henry.—(*Henry lets the oatmeal out.*) Quit that. You just quit that. (*Henry slaps the cup of milk and spills it on the floor.*) That is it, Henry. (*Taking Henry's bib off.*) You get your own food.
HENRY: It spilled!
LLOYD: You did it on purpose.
HENRY: It spilled.
LLOYD: No, it didn't. You spilled it.
HENRY: Clean it!
LLOYD: No, I won't. You clean it. I saw you do it. You clean it.
HENRY: Clean it!
LLOYD: I won't clean it. You clean it.
HENRY: Clean it!
LLOYD: You clean it!
HENRY: Mae. . . ! (*Pause.*) Mae. . . ! (*Pause.*) Mae. . . !
MAE: (*Enters. She carries a bundle of clothes and a cleaning rag.*) What is it?
HENRY: (*Pointing to the milk.*) Look!
MAE: What happened? (*Mae puts the clothes on the bench and stands by Henry with the rag.*)
HENRY: He spilled it!
LLOYD: I didn't spill it! He spilled it!
MAE: So clean it up!
HENRY: Clean it!
LLOYD: I'm going to kill him.
MAE: Kill him if you want.—He can't talk straight any more. (*She starts wiping the oatmeal off Henry.*) Clean up the milk!
HENRY: Clean it!

(*Lloyd takes Henry's bib and starts wiping the milk.*)

MAE: Did you feed the pigs?
LLOYD: Yeah.

MAE: Did Henry eat?

LLOYD: He spilled the milk.

MAE: Did he eat! (*Lloyd doesn't answer.*) Did he eat! (*Pause.*) Did you eat, Henry?

HENRY: I ate.

MAE: He ate. Why didn't you say he ate. (*Mae walks to the left door and opens it.*)

LLOYD: I'm going to kill him.

MAE: (*Stands on the threshold and turns to Lloyd.*) So kill him.

(*They freeze.*)

Scene 14

Mae exits. Lloyd places the bib, the oatmeal cup and spoon, and the tin cup on the mantelpiece. He takes the textbook and sits center. He attempts to read. He first makes the sound of the letter. Then, he speaks the name of the letter and traces it with his finger on the table. Then, he puts the sounds of the letters together. Henry sits to the right facing front. He mimics Lloyd's effort and laughs in silent convulsions.

LLOYD: S.

HENRY: S.

LLOYD: T. St.

HENRY: T. St.

LLOYD: A.

HENRY: A.

LLOYD: Stop that!

HENRY: A.

LLOYD: Stop it, Henry!

HENRY: A.

LLOYD: R. Ar.

HENRY: R. Ar.

LLOYD: Sta.

HENRY: Sta.

LLOYD: Star.

(*The left door opens. Mae stands outside and looks in.*)

HENRY: Star.

LLOYD: F.

HENRY: F.

LLOYD: I. Fi.
HENRY: I. Fi.
LLOYD: S. Fis.
HENRY: S. Fis.
LLOYD: Stop it. Cut it out. Fish.
HENRY: Fish.

(*Mae enters left. She carries a bundle of clothes.*)

LLOYD: Fish.
HENRY: Fish.
MAE: Someone took my money. Who did? (*Neither looks at her.*) Who did!—Did you Lloyd!
LLOYD: I didn't. Fish.
HENRY: Fish.
MAE: Did Henry? Did you take the money, Henry? (*She closes the door.*) Answer me. Did you take the money! Someone took it! You took it, Lloyd. Hand it over.
LLOYD: I didn't take it.
MAE: Hand it over.
LLOYD: I didn't take it!
MAE: Who took it then!
LLOYD: Henry took it.
MAE: (*To Lloyd.*) He didn't take it. He can't walk.
LLOYD: Yes, he can. You know he can. Walk, Henry. Show Mae how you can walk. Walk! He can walk.
MAE: (*Enraged.*) Walk!
HENRY: I can't walk.
LLOYD: You can walk!
MAE: Don't say he can walk, Lloyd. He can't walk. He didn't take the money. (*She notices the book.*) What are you doing with my book? (*He lowers his head. She is perplexed.*) What are you doing? (*She takes the book and holds it protectively.*) Don't mess my book.
HENRY: He was messing it. (*He laughs.*)
MAE: Shut up, Henry.
HENRY: He was saying "Fish." (*He laughs.*)
MAE: Everything turns bad for me.

(*They freeze.*)

Scene 15

Lloyd exits. Mae places the book on the mantelpiece and stands by the down-right corner of the table. Henry walks to the left and sits. His hand is inside his fly. He handles himself.

HENRY: Mae. I still feel desire.—I am sexual.—I have not lost my sexuality.—Mae, make love to me. (*Mae doesn't answer. He continues touching himself.*) You are my wife. I want you. I feel the same desires. I feel the same needs. I have not changed. (*He holds on to the table and begins to stand.*) Mae, I have not stopped wanting you.—I can make love to you.—I can satisfy you. (*Supporting himself on the table, he slides toward her.*) I am potent.—I can make you happy. Kiss me, Mae.—(*He grabs her wrist.*) Tell me you still love me. Kiss me. Let me feel you close to me.—You think a cripple has no feelings.—I'm not crippled in my parts.—It gets hard. (*He puts his right arm around her waist.*) Mae, I love you. (*He holds her tighter. He starts moving his pelvis against her.*) I'm coming. . . . (*He starts sliding down to the floor.*) I'm coming. . . . I'm coming. . . . I'm coming. . . . I'm coming. . . . (*He collapses. She falls on the chair. She stands and leans against the table.*)

MAE: You can walk, Henry. You took my money.

(*They freeze.*)

Scene 16

Mae exits left. Henry is on the floor trying to sit on the chair. Lloyd enters right. He helps Henry up and closes his fly. Mae enters with Henry's box and lifts it up in the air.

HENRY: Don't Mae.
MAE: (*Throwing the box at him.*) Get out!

(*Lloyd exits right.*)

HENRY: Don't throw things at me, Mae!
MAE: You took the money!
HENRY: You hurt me, Mae! You threw that box at me and hurt me!
MAE: You took the money!
HENRY: I didn't take it!
MAE: You took it! Where is it? (*She moves toward him.*)

HENRY: I didn't take it!

(*Mae reaches in his right pocket. She pulls out a wad of bills. She grabs his necktie, turns it back and pulls it down. Lloyd puts his head in through the left door and begins to enter. Mae and Lloyd speak the following speeches at the same time.*)

MAE: I feed you and I take care of you! And you steal from me? You eat my food and you sleep in my bed and you steal from me! You're a pig, Henry. You're worse than Lloyd!

LLOYD: Kill him, Mae! Kill him! Kill him! (*He climbs on the table on all fours.*) He's no good! Kill him, Mae! He's no good! He's a thief!

(*Henry falls off the chair. Mae falls on her knees next to him. Lloyd jumps off the table. He lets out a hysterical laugh.*)

LLOYD: Look he's bleeding! (*He chants and dances.*) Henry's bleeding! Henry's bleeding! Henry's bleeding!
MAE: Shut up, Lloyd!

(*There is silence.*)

HENRY: It was my money. Lloyd never paid me. He never paid me. He never paid me what he owed me.
MAE: You could have let him have it. Just because he takes care of you. You could have let him have your money. He takes care of you.
HENRY: He never paid me.
MAE: (*She looks up to the sky.*) Can't I have a decent life? (*There is a pause.*)
LLOYD: But I love you, Mae.
HENRY: I love you, Mae.

(*They freeze.*)

Scene 17

Lloyd places the box inside the fireplace. He closes the left door. Mae gets the empty box from the fireplace and places it on the right chair. She places the bundle of women's clothes from under the bench on the table. She is packing clothes in the box. Lloyd stands up-left. He watches her. Henry sits left.

MAE: (*As she packs.*) I'm leaving, Lloyd. I'm going somewhere else. I'm leaving you and Henry. Both of you are no good. I got rotten luck. I work too hard and the two of you keep sucking my blood. I'm going to look for a better place to be. (*Lloyd sits on the chair upstage of the table.*) Just a place where the two of you are not sucking my blood. I'm going to find myself a job. And a room to live in. Far away from you. Where I don't have my blood sucked.

LLOYD: Don't go, Mae.

HENRY: Don't go.

MAE: I'm going and that's that.

LLOYD: Where are you going?

MAE: I don't know, Lloyd. I'm just going.

LLOYD: I'll do what you say.

MAE: I don't care what you do. (*Closing the box.*) You do what you want. Henry too. I don't care what he does.

LLOYD: Stay, Mae.

HENRY: Please.

MAE: I'm going. You take care of Henry, Lloyd. (*She goes to the door.*)

LLOYD: Don't go, Mae.

HENRY: Please.

MAE: Goodbye.

(*She exits through the right door and closes the door. Lloyd is still for a few seconds. He then runs to the door, knocking down his chair. He exits.*)

LLOYD: (*Shouting.*) Mae. . . ! (*Henry makes a plaintive sound.*) Mae. . . !

HENRY: Mae. . . !

LLOYD: (*Offstage.*) Mae. . . ! (*Henry makes a plaintive sound.*) Stop, Mae!

HENRY: Stop!

(*Lloyd enters running. He takes the rifle. Henry makes incoherent sounds. Lloyd exits running.*)

LLOYD: Mae. . . ! Stop. . . ! Stop, Mae!

HENRY: Mae. . . !

LLOYD: Mae, stop. . . !

HENRY: Mae. . . !

LLOYD: Mae! Mae! Mae!

(*A shot is heard. There is silence. Another shot is heard.*)

HENRY: (*Plaintively.*) . . . Mae . . .

(*Lloyd appears in threshold carrying Mae. She is drenched in blood and unconscious. Lloyd turns to Henry.*)

LLOYD: She's not leaving, Henry.

(*Henry lets out a whimper. Lloyd places Mae on the table. Mae begins to move.*)

MAE: Like the starfish, I live in the dark and my eyes see only a faint light. It is faint and yet it consumes me. I long for it. I thirst for it. I would die for it. Lloyd, I am dying.

(*Mae collapses. Lloyd sobs. Henry lets out a plaintive cry. They freeze.*)

END

- Knowledge
- cleanliness
- love
- sex

- education
- dissability
- humanness

The Danube

Author's Note:

A tape which follows the language record convention is played where indicated in this script. Each sentence is heard in English, then in Hungarian, then there is enough blank tape for the actors to speak the same line.

The lesson number and title which head the scenes indicated should be heard on the recording in English only and should not be repeated by the actors.

In order to maintain a flow of life on stage through the recorded speeches it is recommended that the actors do not appear to be aware of the recorded voices. This can be achieved as follows:

1) The style of speaking of the recorded voices should be in the style of speaking of recorded language lessons. But the style of speaking of the actors should be naturalistic.

2) The actors should hear and assimilate a line when it is delivered to them, but they should not respond or react to it till it is time for them to reply. If they should react to it immediately but not speak, it would be apparent that the recording is impeding their speaking and that their behavior is not autonomous. It would not be difficult to maintain a liveliness during the recorded interval if the actor imagines the other person elaborating further on what he or she has just said.

3) The actors should deliver their lines with a different sense, a different emphasis, or a different reading from that on the tape.

4) The actors' lines should slightly overlap the recorded Hungarian lines.

This sign in the script "//" indicates where the recorded voices are heard.

———

The Danube was first presented at the 5th Padua Hills Festival, Claremont, California, in 1982 under the title *You Can Swim in the Danube—But the Water is Too Cold.* It was directed by the author with the following cast:

Paul	Leon Martell
Mr. Sandor	Dudley Knight
Eve	Patricia Mattick
Mr. Kovacs/Waiter/Barber	Lee Kissman

Morgan Weisser, Lola Moon Glaudini, and Jessica Wood were also players in this production.

Sets and Costumes: Monica Lorca

Subsequent productions of *The Danube* were done at the Theater for the New City (1983) and The American Place Theatre (1984), where the play was developed in its present form. ———

The set is a playing platform with four vertical posts. Two are on the upstage side of the platform two feet from each side. The other two are on each side of the platform four feet from the downstage side. Painted backdrops, in a style resembling postcards, depict the different locations. A drop with a theatre curtain is hung on the downstage posts. At each change of scenery smoke will go up from three places on the stage floor. The play starts in 1938. However, it soon departs from chronological realism.

The scenes are:

1. *A neighborhood cafe*
2. *On the banks of the Danube*
3. *A restaurant*
4. *A garden*
5. *Paul's room (Bed)*
6. *By a castle*
7. *Paul's room (Doctor)*
8. *Paul's room (Dinner)*
9. *A sanatorium*
10. *Mr. Sandor's living room (Coffee)*
11. *A barbershop*
12. *Mr. Sandor's living room (Blame)*
13. *A puppet stage*
14. *A puppet stage*
15. *A black backdrop (Packing)*

Characters:

Paul Green: A well-meaning American, age 30
Mr. Sandor: A Hungarian bureaucrat, age 50
Eve Sandor: Mr. Sandor's daughter, age 24
Mr. Kovacs: A friend of Mr. Sandor, age 48
The Waiter
The Doctor
The Barber

All the above are members of a well-mannered working class. It is suggested that Mr. Kovacs, the Waiter, the Doctor and the Barber be played by the same actor.

Setting: Budapest, 1938

Scene 1

A neighborhood cafe in Budapest. Mr. Sandor sits at a table. He wears a brown suit, a white shirt and a black tie and shoes. On the table is a shot glass containing spirits and a newspaper which he has folded to a manageable size. Paul approaches him. He wears a tweed jacket and hat, a wool plaid shirt and wool tie and trousers.

ON TAPE: "Unit One. Basic sentences. Paul Green meets Mr. Sandor and his daughter Eve." Also include dialogue in English and Hungarian up to "Are you Hungarian?"

PAUL: //Good afternoon Mr. Sandor.// I believe we met at the Smith's last night.

MR. SANDOR: //Yes, I remember. Your name is Paul Green.

PAUL: //Yes.

MR. SANDOR: (*Standing and shaking Paul's hand.*) //Please, take a seat. (*They sit.*)

PAUL: //Thank you.

MR. SANDOR: //Are you Hungarian?

PAUL: Oh no. I'm from the U.S.

MR. SANDOR: What is new in the U.S.?

PAUL: The weather is bad.

MR. SANDOR: Is that so?

PAUL: Yes, we have not had good weather.

MR. SANDOR: I see.

PAUL: And how is the weather in Budapest?

MR. SANDOR: It has been bad. We have not had good weather. Are you visiting Budapest?

PAUL: No. I have come here to study and work. My company has sent me here.

MR. SANDOR: What is your line of work, Mr. Green?

PAUL: Metal production.

MR. SANDOR: I am glad to hear that. I have a son and two daughters and they all study. The eldest, my son, works and studies; my eldest daughter studies and she is not working presently. And my youngest daughter is studying and she has not yet started to work.

PAUL: What do they study?

MR. SANDOR: My eldest daughter studies German, English and Hungarian. The youngest studies accounting.

PAUL: And what does your son study?

MR. SANDOR: My son is an aviator and he studies German. Some say German is the language of the future. Others say English is the language of the future. That is why Eve studies both.

PAUL: Hungarian is the language of the future. (*They laugh.*)

MR. SANDOR: Hungarian may be the language of poetry but not of the future. I don't see very much poetry in the future. Do you?

PAUL: No, I don't. • bleak outlook

MR. SANDOR: You must be a practical man.

PAUL: Yes. I think so.

MR. SANDOR: So is my son. He flies a commercial plane. Yesterday he went up with his youngest daughter. Have you ever been up in a plane, Mr. Green?

PAUL: No, I haven't.

MR. SANDOR: I haven't either. One day I may go up with my son. I am looking forward to being so high up in the air that a house would look like a speck in the distance. Would you care for a cigarette? (*He offers Paul a cigarette.*)

PAUL: (*Taking it.*) Thanks. Hungarian cigarette?

MR. SANDOR: No, this is a German cigarette. It is from a German factory like airplanes and shoes. • outsourcing

PAUL: Thank you very much. (*He puts the cigarette in his pocket.*) Thanks.

MR. SANDOR: What have you seen in Budapest?

PAUL: I have not seen very much yet. Since I arrived I have worked and I have attended school. I also spent time looking for a place to live.

MR. SANDOR: Have you found a place?

PAUL: Yes, I have found a room in a hotel on Maria Street.

(*Eve enters. She wears a lightweight two-piece suit. She stands at the door looking out.*)

MR. SANDOR: Here is my daughter Eve. Eve, please come here. (*Eve approaches.*) I should like to introduce Mr. Paul Green from the U.S.

*recorded voices are no longer heard but this
simplistic speech lingers on*

(*Paul stands.*)

EVE: (*Shaking hands.*) Glad to meet you.

PAUL: Thank you.

EVE: But, please, take a seat. (*They sit.*)

PAUL: Thanks. Very gladly.

EVE: Do you understand Hungarian? I speak English.

PAUL: I understand Hungarian.

MR. SANDOR: She understands German, English and Hungarian.

EVE: Do you understand German?

PAUL: I don't understand German.

EVE: But you speak Hungarian very well.

PAUL: I studied Hungarian in the U.S. My firm had me take special courses in Hungarian. They have a Hungarian affiliated firm.

(*She offers him a cigarette.*)

EVE: Would you care for a cigarette?

PAUL: (*Taking it.*) Thanks. (*Putting it in his pocket.*) Thank you very much. I believe I have seen you on Baross Street, Miss Sandor.

EVE: Oh, yes. We live on Baross Street.

PAUL: I live on Maria Street.

EVE: We live near each other. Maria Street crosses Baross Street.

PAUL: How far is my house from yours?

EVE: Your house is five minutes from ours.

PAUL: I saw you in the bakery.

EVE: I go there each day. I buy bread in the bakery on Baross Street.

PAUL: How fortunate.

EVE: Yes. Have you lived here long?

PAUL: Not very long. I have lived here two weeks.

EVE: This is not the most elegant part of Budapest. But it is very convenient. We are near the shops and it is economical. We have nice parks and the streets are clean.

PAUL: Maybe you'll be so good as to show me the parks, Miss Sandor.

EVE: I'll be glad to.

PAUL: Thank you.

EVE: I am free in the early evening, before dinner.

PAUL: Would you be free tomorrow at this time?

EVE: Yes.

PAUL: How very fortunate. (*To Mr. Sandor.*) Mr. Sandor, at what time is dinner in Budapest?

MR. SANDOR: Dinner is around eight p.m. Breakfast around eight o'clock. Lunch between twelve and one.

EVE: Sometimes we eat a morning snack too.

PAUL: What do you eat for breakfast as a rule?

EVE: For breakfast, we drink tea or coffee. Sometimes we eat an egg too, with bread or a roll and butter.

MR. SANDOR: In the afternoon, women especially drink coffee. They customarily do. In the morning before work men usually drink palinka in a cafe.

PAUL: Will you be free tomorrow till eight, Miss Sandor?

EVE: I will be free tomorrow till eight. I usually go home at seven. But tomorrow my father will cook. On Thursdays he likes to cook goulash. My father is a very good cook.

PAUL: Are you a good cook, Miss Sandor?

EVE: I am also a good cook. Do you like to cook, Mr. Green?

PAUL: I am not a very good cook. I only know how to make eggs, toast, boiled potatoes and a steak. What forms of entertainment are there in Budapest, Miss Sandor?

EVE: In Budapest there is dancing. There is swimming in the baths. There is music in the parks and concert halls. There are picnics in the countryside and there are theatres and movies.

PAUL: Do you enjoy the movies, Mr. Sandor?

MR. SANDOR: I do.

PAUL: Do you, Miss Sandor?

EVE: Oh yes.

PAUL: (*To Eve.*) May I invite you to the movies?

EVE: Yes, thank you.

PAUL: Mr. Sandor, would you come to the movies also?

MR. SANDOR: I would be glad to. I often go to the movies.

PAUL: Would you like to go tonight?

MR. SANDOR: Not tonight. I am expecting my friend Mr. Kovacs tonight. He is coming for dinner. But Eve may join you. She likes the movies very much.

PAUL: (*To Eve.*) Do you know at what time the movie starts?

EVE: I believe it begins at eight.

PAUL: Do you know what is playing?

EVE: We can look in the evening paper.

MR. SANDOR: This is the morning paper.

EVE: It is not evening yet.

PAUL: I will bring the paper when I come.

MR. SANDOR: We must leave now. (*Giving Paul a card.*) 9 Baross Street. First floor. Second door to the left.

PAUL: Thank you.

(*Mr. Sandor and Eve stand. Paul stands.*)

MR. SANDOR: We have a dining room, two bedrooms, a kitchen and a bathroom. The bathroom is very good because it has hot and cold water.

listing rooms for vocabulary

(*Paul gives Mr. Sandor his own card.*)

PAUL: This is my card.
MR. SANDOR: (*Giving the card to Eve.*) Thank you.
PAUL: Thank you.
MR. SANDOR, PAUL, EVE: Good bye.

(*Eve and Mr. Sandor exit left. Paul exits right. "The Blue Danube" is heard. As the scenery is changed, smoke goes up from the stage floor.*)

Scene 2

On the banks of the Danube. There is a view of Budapest. There is a bench. Mr. Sandor, Eve, Mr. Kovacs and Paul enter.

ON TAPE: "Unit Two. Basic sentences. Mr. Sandor, Kovacs, Eve and Paul discuss their relatives by the Danube." The scene is performed without a tape.

KOVACS: Of my sons, one is a doctor, one is a soldier, and the other is a clerk.
EVE: When I have a son, I would like for him to be a teacher.
KOVACS: I always wanted one of my sons to be a soldier, like my father. And one did become a soldier.
MR. SANDOR: Was that Stephen?
KOVACS: No, Stephen is not a soldier.
MR. SANDOR: He is a clerk.
KOVACS: He works in a factory. George is the soldier. What does your brother do, Mr. Green?
PAUL: My brother is a farmer and so is my father. And my sister is a nurse.
KOVACS: I am a tailor.
PAUL: And is your brother a tailor too?
KOVACS: No, my brother isn't a tailor. He's a shoemaker. He makes shoes. I have one cousin who is a tailor, and another who is a mason.
MR. SANDOR: My father's father was a mason. But he also did plumbing like his cousin.
EVE: My father's cousin was a seamstress and her daughter was a teacher. They live in Paks. Is your niece married, Mr. Kovacs?

KOVACS: Yes. She's married. Her husband is a carpenter. He has his own shop. And she is a stenographer. Today women work as well as men.

MR. SANDOR: Yes, my brother works in an armament factory and his wife works in the same plant.

KOVACS: My nephew also works in the same factory. And his brother is a waiter. He works the early shift.

MR. SANDOR: I am a clerk in the custom house. I have worked there since I was young.

KOVACS: I have a nephew who is a barber. He owns his own shop. Another cousin is a doctor. He is a good doctor. Well, good bye now. I want to buy cigarettes before the stores close. (*To Eve.*) Good bye. (*To Paul.*) I enjoyed the movies, Mr. Green. I like American movies.

PAUL: Thank you.

KOVACS: Good bye.

MR. SANDOR: I'll go with you. Good bye.

ALL: Good bye.

(*Kovacs and Mr. Sandor exit. There is a pause.*)

PAUL: The city is very beautiful.

EVE: Yes, it is. Budapest lies on two sides of the Danube. Buda is on the right side. Pest is on the left. Between the two towns there are six bridges. From the mountains of Buda you can see Pest. On the Pest side is Parliament. The cathedral is not far. Budapest is full of baths. For example the one on Margaret Island. That bath is very beautiful. There's hot and cold water. The island lies in the middle of the Danube.

PAUL: Eve, come with me to a cafe. There's one not far from my hotel.

EVE: Let's go. (*They start to go.*) You can bathe in the Danube but the water is too cold. The weather is bad. It has changed.

break from monotony

(*They exit. "The Blue Danube" is heard. As the scenery is changed, smoke goes up from the stage floor.*)

Scene 3

The restaurant. It is a working class restaurant. There is a table and two chairs. The table is set with glasses, silver dishes and napkins. Paul and Eve enter. They are cheerful.

ON TAPE: "Unit Three. Basic sentences. Paul and Eve go to the restaurant." Also include dialogue in English and Hungarian up to "Yes, *here's one."*

PAUL: //Here comes the waiter.
WAITER: //What do you wish?
PAUL: //Have you a table for two?
WAITER: //Yes, here's one.

(They sit. The Waiter gets a water pitcher and a menu. He walks to the table, gives them the menu and pours water.)

WAITER: Will you have lunch?
PAUL: Yes, both of us.
EVE: What soup do you have?
WAITER: Beef broth.
PAUL: Bring two beef broth.
EVE: What sort of meat is there?
WAITER: There is chicken with paprika. There is cold and hot ham.
PAUL: I'd like fish.
WAITER: I'm very sorry but there is no fish.
EVE: Then bring the chicken.
WAITER: Would you like some wine?
EVE: I only want a glass of water.
PAUL: I would like a glass of white wine. *(The Waiter exits.)*
PAUL: Where shall we go this afternoon?
EVE: We could go to a museum.
PAUL: Which museum?
EVE: The economic museum is very interesting.
PAUL: Where is the economic museum?
EVE: Not very far. *(The Waiter enters with soup and puts it on the table.)*
PAUL: Thank you.
WAITER: With pleasure.
PAUL: Shall we go by car?
EVE: The streetcar is much cheaper. And you can see the town from the window. One comes every minute.
PAUL: I would also like to do some shopping.
EVE: What would you like to buy?
PAUL: A present for my sister. Another for my mother. I also have to buy something for my brother and presents for my niece and nephew.
EVE: . . . Paul . . . *(Paul looks at Eve.)* Are you leaving Budapest?
PAUL: Yes. I have been asked to return to the U.S.

(There is a sudden sound of plaintive music which continues playing through the following dialogue. Paul and Eve are distressed.)

EVE: Oh, no.

PAUL: Yes.

EVE: How soon?

PAUL: In two weeks.

EVE: Please, don't go.

PAUL: I don't want to go.

EVE: Please, don't go.

PAUL: I want to stay.

EVE: It will never be the same without you. I feel cold. Is it winter yet? (*The Waiter enters with the menu.*)

WAITER: We have no more chicken. Would you like the hot ham?

EVE: No, thank you.

WAITER: Would you like some hot ham?

PAUL: No, thank you.

WAITER: You should eat when you can. The crops have not been good. Would you like some dessert.

PAUL: What desserts do you have?

WAITER: We have apple pie, ice cream, and fresh fruit. May I suggest the fresh fruit?

(*The Waiter and Eve freeze. The music stops.*)

PAUL: (*Speaking rapidly.*) I came from a country where we hear out suggestions. We invented the suggestion box. The best suggestion may come from the least expected place. We value ideas. We don't hesitate to put ideas to practice. We consider ideas that are given to us. We don't hold back our suggesting of ideas for fear of appearing foolish. We are not afraid to appear foolish, as good ideas disguise themselves in foolishness. We are not afraid to appear foolish. We are the foolish race.

EVE: (*As if in a trance.*) I'll have fresh fruit.

WAITER: Sir?

PAUL: I'll have fresh fruit.

WAITER: You are foolish but oh how fast you move forward.

EVE: Please, let's go to a cafe.

(*As she stands, her chair falls to the floor. Paul picks up the chair and turns to where the Waiter exited.*)

PAUL: Waiter, please, give me the bill.

(*The Waiter enters. Eve faints.*)

WAITER: You don't want fresh fruit?

He shattered their reality!

PAUL: No, thank you.

(*The Waiter starts writing the bill. Paul starts to pay. He is distressed and disoriented. He drops bills and coins, picks them up, puts a bill on the Waiter's tray, takes money from another pocket, drops more coins and bills, and puts two bills on the Waiter's tray.*)

WAITER: Thank you. (*The Waiter moves to the up left corner and stands in a very straight stylized position. Paul picks up Eve's napkin, puts it on the table, and freezes with knees bent in an almost squatting position. Eve also freezes. The Waiter speaks rapidly in a declamatory manner. Through the course of the speech he gradually raises the tray which he holds with both hands in front of him.*) We are concerned with quality. That which is lasting. Craftsmanship. A thing of quality always ends up being heavy. We have preferred quality to anything else. We wish for things to last but we tire of them. We are buried under the stones of buildings, iron grates, heavy shoes, woolen garments, heavy sheets, foods that smell potent like the caves in the black forest. Hands that cut, knead and saw and measure and chisel and sweat into everything we see. Pots that are too heavy to use. Shoes that delay our walk. Sheets that make our sleep a slumber.— Americans sleep light and wake up briskly. You create life each day. Here, the little trousers a boy wears to school are waiting for him at the store before he is born. We are dark. Americans are bright.—You crave mobility. The car. You move from city to city so as not to grow stale. You don't stay too long in a place. A person who lives too long in the same house is suspect. It's someone who is held back. Friction keeps a stone polished. Mobility. You are alert. You get in and out of cars limberly. That is your grace. Our grace is weighty. Not yours. You worship the long leg and loose hip joint. How else to jump in and out of cars. You dress light. You travel light. You are light on your feet. You are light hearted and a light heart is a pump that brings you to motion. You aim to alight, throw the load overboard. Alight the flight. You are responsible. That is not a burden. You are responsible to things that move forward. You are responsible to the young. Not so much to the old. The old do not move forward. You will find a way for the old to move forward, have them join in your thrust. Solving a problem is not a burden to you. A problem solved is a lifting of a burden. Egyptians lifted heavy stones to build monuments. You lift them to get rid of heavy stones. Get rid of them! Obstacles! You are efficient. You simplify life. Paper work. Your forms are shorter, so is your period of obligation. Work. Your hours are shorter and you have more time to sit on the lawn in your cotton trousers. (*He lowers the tray. Eve comes to.*

Paul helps her up.)
EVE: Let's take a streetcar.
PAUL: Let's go.

(They exit. Music plays. The Waiter exits. As the scenery is changed smoke goes up from the stage floor.)

Scene 4

In the garden. There are dried leaves. There is a cement pillar, the top of which is cut at a slant with a cloth sculpted over it. The word "True" is engraved on the base. The sound tape contains only the Hungarian phrases.

EVE: //This may be the last time I come here.// Here is where I first kissed you.// I kissed you that day, you know.// I kissed you because I could not help myself.// Now again I try to exert control over myself// and I can't.// I try to appear content and I can't.// I know I look distressed.// I feel how my face quivers. And my blood feels thin.// And I can hardly breathe. And my skin feels dry.// I have no power to show something other than what I feel.// I am destroyed. And even if I try,// my lips will not smile.// Instead I cling to you and make it harder for you.// Leave now.// Leave me here looking at the leaves.// Good bye.// If I don't look at you it may be that I can let you go.

(Paul kisses her. Music plays. Lights fade. As the scenery is changed smoke goes up from the stage floor.)

Scene 5

Paul's bedroom. It is almost dawn. Eve and Paul lie on a cot by the window. Eve's head lies on Paul's chest. They are covered with a sheet. The sound tape includes the complete dialogue in both English and Hungarian.

EVE: Silence . . . // Silence . . . // Adieu . . . // Adieu . . . // Hold me this last time.// And kiss me.// Kiss me one more time. *(They kiss. She puts her head down on his chest again and caresses his eyes with her fingers.)* //Adieu . . . Farewell to your eyes.// I will never see them.// Farewell, sweet eyes.
PAUL: //This cannot be.// I will stay.// I must stay.// Marry me, sweet

Eve.// I will marry you.
EVE: //Oh, Paul, you love me.// You do. You love me.// You do.// You will be happy since I love you so.
PAUL: //I'll never say adieu again.

(The sky outside the window is lit.)

PAUL: //Look, here is the dawn.

(Lights fade. Music plays. As the scenery is changed, smoke goes up from the stage floor.)

Scene 6

By a castle. Eve looks out to the left. There is the sound of a fox-trot. She dances a little in place. Paul enters with two glasses. He puts the glasses down and takes her by the waist. They dance for a while. The music ends. They continue dancing. The scene is performed without a language tape.

EVE: The music ended.
PAUL: If I tried, I could not stop.

(Lights fade. There is the sound of Eve's panting. The lights come up. Eve is standing against the wall. She holds a drink in her hand. Her mouth and eyes are wide open. Paul is lying on the floor. His body is contorted. His face is in a grimace. There is an eerie sound.)

EVE: . . . Paul!—

(Lights fade. There is music. As the scenery is changed, smoke goes up from the stage floor.)

Scene 7

It is Paul's room. There is a table and two chairs. Paul has a blood pressure device attached to his arm. He is sitting on the upstage side of the table. The Doctor sits to the right. There is a doctor's case on the floor to the right of the Doctor. They both suffer slight physical contortions, an ankle, a shoulder, a few fingers. All other characters suffer the same contortions. As the play advances these contortions will become more extreme.

ON TAPE: *"Unit Seven. Basic sentences. Paul Green is examined by the Doctor." The sound tape includes the complete dialogue in both English and Hungarian.*

DOCTOR: //Your blood is thin.// Have you been eating well?

PAUL: //Yes. (*The Doctor looks into Paul's eyes.*)

DOCTOR: //Come here, closer to the light. (*They go upstage to the window, he looks again at his eye. He takes his pulse.*) //Let me see your tongue. (*Paul sticks his tongue out. The Doctor puts a tongue depressor on it.*) //Say ahh.

PAUL: Ahh. (*The Doctor walks back to the table.*)

DOCTOR: (*Thoughtfully.*) //It's nothing serious.// Sit down.// (*Paul sits.*) What you have is common.// Thin blood.// A white throat.// The eyes secrete mucus.// You feel very ill.// And yet the symptoms are not serious.// Do you excrete normally?

PAUL: //No.

DOCTOR: //This is common.

PAUL: //What is causing it? (*The Doctor writes.*)

DOCTOR: //Does your wife suffer from this too?

PAUL: //I think so.

DOCTOR: //Not as severely?

PAUL: //No.

DOCTOR: (*Still writing.*) //Take a train to Fured.// There, repose yourself.// Drink this tonic four times a day.// Sleep. And don't worry. (*He takes his bag and stands up to leave. He takes a last look at Paul's eyes, ears, teeth. He feels his forehead. He looks at his fingernails. He then takes a handkerchief from his pocket and puts it over Paul's nose.*) //Blow your nose on this. (*Paul does. The Doctor looks at the secretion in the handkerchief, puts it in his pocket and exits. Lights fade. There is music. As the scenery is changed, smoke goes up from the stage floor.*)

Scene 8

Paul's room. There is a table set with soup dishes. Mr. Sandor sits on the up right side. Mr. Kovacs sits on the down left side. Paul stands stage right. Eve stands stage left.

ON TAPE: *"Unit Eight. Basic sentences. Paul and Eve Green invite Mr. Sandor and Mr. Kovacs for dinner." The scene is performed without a language tape.*

Eve starts to exit left. Paul follows her.

EVE: Please, you don't need to come. I can serve.

(*Eve exits. Paul follows her.*)

KOVACS: (*To Mr. Sandor.*) Do you know how to cook?

MR. SANDOR: Of course. When my wife died I learned to cook. Eve was only seven. The boy and I did the housework.

KOVACS: I also know how to cook and so does my younger brother. We Hungarians like good food. (*Eve and Paul enter carrying soup in metal cups. They pour the soup and sit, Eve on the down side, Paul on the up left side.*) Do you know how to cook, Mr. Green?

PAUL: I only know how to make eggs, toast, boil potatoes and cook a steak; fried or grilled in the oven or barbequed.

KOVACS: That is plenty.

PAUL: It would not be interesting to eat this every day.

KOVACS: What?

PAUL: Eggs, toast, boiled potatoes and steak.

KOVACS: That would be too much.

PAUL: Do you know how to cook, Mr. Kovacs?

KOVACS: I know how to make chicken paprika and beef goulash.

MR. SANDOR: I make cabbage soup with beef.

EVE: Is the soup good?

KOVACS: It is good.

MR. SANDOR: It is as good as I ever had.

KOVACS: I have a feeling Honved is not winning today.

MR. SANDOR: I think Honved is winning.

KOVACS: How could Honved win? It is not a good team.

MR. SANDOR: Honved is a very good team. It is better than MTK.

KOVACS: Oh no. MTK is better than Honved.

MR. SANDOR: Not at all. Honved is the leading team. It wins all the time.

KOVACS: It is not better. It is worse. They just have better luck.

MR. SANDOR: You don't win soccer with luck, Kovacs.

KOVACS: Honved does.

MR. SANDOR: Paul, what is it Americans call a bad loser? Is Kovacs a bad loser . . . is he? (*Paul smiles. Mr. Sandor speaks to Kovacs.*) You're a bad loser.

KOVACS: Do you play soccer, Paul?

PAUL: In the U.S., we don't play soccer. We play football, baseball and basketball.

KOVACS: (*To Mr. Sandor.*) I never knew that. Did you know that, Henry?

MR. SANDOR: I did. Football, baseball and basketball are American games. Soccer is not.

(*Paul faints. Eve stands and looks at him alarmed.*)

EVE: He has not been well. (*Pause.*) And neither have I.

(*Mr. Sandor and Kovacs look at each other and lower their heads. Lights fade. There is music. As the scenery is changed, smoke goes up from the stage floor.*)

Scene 9

A sanatorium. There is a small desk and chair. To the left there is a cot. On the back wall there is a moonlit mountain peak. Paul is wearing pajamas, a robe, and slippers. He is at the desk writing.

PAUL: Dearest Eve. How are you? Have you missed me? What is new? How is work? I am still under constant observation. I must see the doctor at two each day. I am always hopeful. The doctors say that my teeth have caused it. It is not true. There is something in the air. It is natural I feel sad. Nothing I do makes me feel right. All my hours go into longing for you and the hour of my return. I have little hope. What do you think? All my love. Paul.

(*Lights fade. There is music. Smoke goes up from the stage floor. The stage is lit. Paul lies on the cot. He is covered with a sheet. A sound tape contains only the Hungarian phrases.*)

PAUL: //Eve, I feel much worse.// I have a high fever.// My vision is blurred. (*Eve appears by Paul's side. He holds her.*) //Who knows why, but suddenly I am here next to you.// I just left Fured and suddenly here I am next to you.// Write to the captain in regard to this.// Tell him that I cannot bear it any longer.// That I am dying.// That I am going mad.// Tell him that he must release me.// That I cannot be of any use to Hungary.// That I am a peaceful man. (*Short pause.*) //Oh, no. I know that is not possible.// Every man must do his share. (*He cries.*) //There is no point.// We are all useless to Hungary.// We cannot save her.// Oh, Hungary, we cannot save you.

(*Lights fade. There is music. Smoke goes up from the stage floor. The stage is lit. Eve is sitting at the table writing and Paul lies in bed unconscious. The following is performed without a language tape.*)

EVE: Paul Green, private, front line. A long time has passed and things are not any clearer. I know there is no front line and I know there is no war. I wish there were one. A war would end and you would return to me. I don't know where you are. You are where I am but never at the same time. My dearest, life escapes from us like blood out of a wound. Will we ever be whole again and in each other's arms? All my love, Eve.

(*Lights fade. There is music. As the scenery is changed, smoke goes up from the stage floor.*)

Scene 10

Mr. Sandor's living room. There is a table and two chairs. Mr. Sandor enters right. He carries a tray with a coffee pot and two cups. He stands with his back to the left, places the tray on the table and pours. All characters will wear goggles from here on. Their speech will be progressively convoluted. Their skin will show reddish spots as if of burns. Their clothes appear to have been exposed to ash dust and strange drippings.

ON TAPE: "*Unit Ten. Basic sentences. Paul Green visits Mr. Sandor. They discuss the weather.*" *The scene is performed without a language tape.*

MR. SANDOR: Hello, Paul. (*Paul enters, Mr. Sandor turns.*) Would you like some coffee?

PAUL: Yes, thanks. (*Paul sits. Mr. Sandor gives Paul a cup, and takes the other to his chair. He sits.*) Perhaps tomorrow the weather will be good.

MR. SANDOR: Yes, the weather is bad. Perhaps tomorrow the weather will be good.

PAUL: In the morning I was warm. Now in the evening it's cold. Where's Eve?

MR. SANDOR: She went to town.

PAUL: But it's raining. In the winter she works. In the summer she studies. I haven't seen her since spring.

MR. SANDOR: Would you have a cigarette?

PAUL: Yes, please. (*Mr. Sandor gives him a cigarette.*)

MR. SANDOR: Of course. Here's a match. How's the coffee?

PAUL: Very good. (*Paul turns suddenly.*) I think it's snowing.

MR. SANDOR: I don't think so. In the fall it doesn't snow.

PAUL: I hope so. This year was bad enough. I'd like some more coffee.

MR. SANDOR: Certainly. (*Mr. Sandor starts to pour.*)

PAUL: Thanks. What time is it?

MR. SANDOR: Not six yet. Five.

PAUL: There's time for a movie from six to eight.

MR. SANDOR: It's raining very hard.

PAUL: That's true.

MR. SANDOR: (*Offering him another pack of cigarettes.*) Have another cigarette. (*Handing him matches.*) Here is a match. (*Mr. Sandor sits.*) There's still more coffee.

PAUL: This cigarette is wet.

MR. SANDOR: Oh, I beg your pardon. (*Handing him a cigarette.*) Here's another one. You look much better.

PAUL: I am better.

MR. SANDOR: Is Fured a good hospital?

PAUL: Yes, very good. (*Paul looks in the cup.*) What's this? (*Mr. Sandor looks in the cup.*)

MR. SANDOR: Oh, I beg your pardon. (*Mr. Sandor takes an amorphous black object from the cup and looks at it carefully. He puts it in his pocket and sits.*)

PAUL: This coffee is cold. It may be my last cup and it's cold. Which is the way to the toilet? (*Mr. Sandor points to the up left corner.*)

MR. SANDOR: The toilet is to the left.

(*Paul exits. Eve enters from the up right corner and walks to the down left center.*)

EVE: Where is Paul?

MR. SANDOR: I haven't seen him since yesterday.

EVE: Paul . . .

(*Lights fade. There is music. As the scenery is changed, smoke goes up from the stage floor.*)

Scene 11

The barbershop. The Barber sits on a chair on the left. Paul enters stage right, takes a few steps and stops. He wears a brown-green shirt and tie and a band around his arm.

ON TAPE: *"Unit Eleven. Basic sentences. Paul Green goes to the barbershop." The sound tape contains only the Hungarian phrases.*

PAUL: //Please, cut my hair.

BARBER: //Please, take a seat. (*Paul sits. The Barber puts a white cloth around his neck.*) //Are you Hungarian?

PAUL: //No. I am from the United States.

BARBER: //Are you a soldier?

PAUL: //Why yes. (*Paul lifts the cloth.*) //Look at my clothes.

BARBER: //Shall I cut it short in the back?

PAUL: //Please.

(*The Barber cuts Paul's hair. Neither speaks for awhile. Paul looks front.*)

PAUL: //. . . What's this. . . ? //Eve is coming. . . . //She's coming. . . . (*Turning to look at Eve.*) //. . . Eve. . . . (*The Barber turns Paul's head down. He cuts his hair. Eve appears on the up right corner.*)

BARBER: (*Speaking close to Paul's ear. He loses control progressively. He goes on his knees and grabs Paul by the leg.*) //Tell me.// Is it permitted?// For me to ask you.// Please, tell me.// What does one say?// I want?// I want milk?// Please, give me beer?// Meat?// I'm very hungry?// It is the heart of the nation.// It is cold.// The earth is cold.//

PAUL: (*Standing abruptly.*) //I'm very sorry.// I have to go now.// How much does a haircut cost?

BARBER: //This was a plain haircut.// The price is fifty filler.

PAUL: //That's cheap enough.// Have you cigarettes or matches?

BARBER: //I'm sorry but we have no cigarettes or matches.// We only cut hair and shave.// Would you like a shave, sir?

PAUL: (*Handing money to the Barber.*) //No, thank you. That's cheap enough. (*He turns his head towards Eve.*)

EVE: //Let's go.

(*Eve exits. Paul turns towards the exit slowly. He lifts his arm as if reaching for Eve. He has lost her. He exits. Lights fade. There is music. As the scenery is changed, smoke goes up from the stage floor.*)

Scene 12

Eve lies on a blanket on the floor down right. There is a table and chair next to her. Mr. Sandor sits on a chair up left. He sleeps. Paul enters. He is in his underwear. He carries a drawer with clothes, places it on the floor and walks to Eve. The scene is performed without a language tape.

PAUL: Eve, I'm leaving. I can't take this any longer. You take care of the place or burn it if you want. I don't care what you do.

EVE: Why don't you take me with you? (*He sits.*)

PAUL: If you go, we'll never get anywhere. It is you who has polluted me. I am clean of body and mind.

EVE: That's not so. I have not polluted you.

PAUL: It is you who have caused all the trouble.

EVE: You are losing your brain, Paul. You are talking like a machine. You are saying what machines say.

PAUL: It must be true if machines say it. (*She screams and hits him repeatedly.*) I am sorry, Eve. I don't know what made me say that. (*He hits the table with his fist. It breaks apart. He cries.*) I didn't mean any of it. I don't have a mind. And I don't have a soul.

MR. SANDOR: (*Startled as if awakened from a nightmare. He remains so through the following scene.*) What happened!

EVE: Paul got angry, father, and he smashed the table. (*Eve has a coughing attack.*)

MR. SANDOR: Is she ill!

PAUL: Why do you ask that?

MR. SANDOR: She's coughing!

PAUL: She always coughs.

MR. SANDOR: What's wrong with that!

PAUL: Nothing. She coughs, I throw up, and you have diarrhea.

MR. SANDOR: Let's call a doctor!

(*Paul emits a loud and plaintive sound. Lights fade. There is music. As the scenery is changed, smoke goes up from the stage floor.*)

Scene 13

There is a theatre curtain placed on the downstage posts. A puppet stand is placed on stage. On the floor of the puppet stage down right is a blanket. To the left of the blanket and facing it is a chair. To the right of the chair is a breakaway table. On the up left corner is a chair. Paul, Eve, and Mr. Sandor operate puppets whose appearance is identical to theirs. The following scene, which is the same as scene 12, is performed by the puppets.

PAUL: Eve, I'm leaving. I can't take this any longer. You take care of the place or burn it if you want. I don't care what you do.

EVE: Why don't you take me with you? (*He sits.*)

PAUL: If you go, we'll never get anywhere. It is you who has polluted me. I am clean of body and mind.

EVE: That's not so. I have not polluted you.

PAUL: It is you who have caused all the trouble.

EVE: You are losing your brain, Paul. You are talking like a machine. You are saying what machines say.

PAUL: It must be true if machines say it. (*She screams and hits him repeatedly.*) I am sorry, Eve. I don't know what made me say that. (*He hits the table with his fist. It breaks apart. He cries.*) I didn't mean any of it. I don't have a mind. And I don't have a soul.

MR. SANDOR: (*Startled as if awakened from a nightmare. He remains so through the following scene.*) What happened!

EVE: Paul got angry, father, and he smashed the table. (*Eve has a coughing attack.*)

MR. SANDOR: Is she ill!

PAUL: Why do you ask that?

MR. SANDOR: She's coughing!

PAUL: She always coughs.

MR. SANDOR: What's wrong with that!

PAUL: Nothing. She coughs, I throw up, and you have diarrhea.

MR. SANDOR: Let's call a doctor!

(*Paul emits a loud and plaintive sound. Lights fade. There is music. As the scenery is changed, smoke goes up from the stage floor.*)

Scene 14

The actors set up for another puppet scene. There is a table center and a chair to the left and facing it. There are two drawers on the floor against the back wall, one to the right and one to the left. The puppet representing Eve sits at the table. The puppet representing Paul enters.

ON TAPE: "Unit Thirteen. Basic sentences. Paul and Eve pack their suitcase." The scene is performed without a language tape.

PAUL: Eve.

EVE: Yes.

PAUL: Let's go.

EVE: Yes.

(*Paul gets a suitcase and puts it on the table. They each get the items of clothing indicated in the script from the drawers and put them in the suitcase.*)

EVE: Stockings. Five pairs of underpants.

PAUL: Eight pairs of socks.

EVE: Five shirts. Three blouses.

PAUL: Trousers.
EVE: Shorts. Six pairs of shorts. A skirt. A dress.
PAUL: Handkerchiefs. Seven handkerchiefs.
EVE: Everything is here.
PAUL: Let's go.

(*Mr. Sandor enters.*)

MR. SANDOR: What's this?
EVE: Please, father, come with us.
MR. SANDOR: Don't go. (*Eve embraces Mr. Sandor.*)
EVE: Good bye, father. (*Walking to Paul.*) Good bye.

(*Lights fade. There is music. As the scenery is changed, smoke goes up from the stage floor. The puppet stage is removed.*)

Scene 15

Mr. Sandor's livingroom. There is a table center and a chair to the left. Eve sits on the chair. Paul enters. They are both in a state of physical and emotional restraint which hampers their speech and movement.

ON TAPE: "Unit Fourteen. Basic sentences. Paul and Eve Green pack their suitcase." The scene is performed without a language tape.

PAUL: Eve.
EVE: Yes.
PAUL: Let's go.
EVE: Yes. (*Paul gets a suitcase and puts it on the table. They each get the items of clothing indicated in the script from the drawers and put them in the suitcase.*) Stockings. Five pairs of underpants.
PAUL: Eight pairs of socks.
EVE: Five shirts. Three blouses.
PAUL: Trousers.
EVE: Shorts. Six pairs of shorts. A skirt. A dress.
PAUL: Handkerchiefs. Seven handkerchiefs.
EVE: Everything is here.
PAUL: Let's go.
EVE: (*Taking a revolver from the suitcase.*) What's this?
PAUL: (*Reaching for the gun.*) A gun. (*First she resists. Then she releases it. He puts it in his pocket. Mr. Sandor enters.*)
MR. SANDOR: What's this?

PAUL: (*Taking the suitcase.*) Good bye.

EVE: (*Embracing Mr. Sandor.*) Good bye, father.

MR. SANDOR: Don't go.

EVE: Please come with us.

MR. SANDOR: I live here and work here. My family lives here.

EVE: Please, father, come with us.

MR. SANDOR: It doesn't matter, Eve. There's no place to go.

EVE: Good bye. (*Eve walks downstage and speaks front.*) My Danube, you are my wisdom. My river that comes to me, to my city, my Budapest . . . I say good bye. As I die, my last thought is of you, my sick friend. Here is your end. Here is my hand. I don't know myself apart from you. I don't know you apart from myself. This is the hour. We die at last, my Danube. Good bye. (*She joins Paul. They start to exit right.*)

MR. SANDOR: Eve!

(*There is a brilliant white flash of light. Black out.*)

END

The Conduct of Life

To Julian Beck
in memory of his courageous life
(1925-1985)

The Conduct of Life was first produced at Theater for the New City, 162 2nd Avenue, New York City, on February 21, 1985. It was directed by the author with the following cast:

Orlando	Pedro Garrido
Leticia	Crystal Field
Alejo	Hermann Lademann
Olimpia	Alba Oms
Nena	Sheila Dabney

Sets: T. Owen Baumgartner
Lights: Anne E. Militello
Costumes: Sally Lesser

CHARACTERS:

Orlando: An army lieutenant at the start of the play. A lieutenant commander soon after.
Leticia: His wife, ten years his elder.
Alejo: A lieutenant commander. Their friend.
Nena: A destitute girl of twelve.
Olimpia: A servant.

A Latin American country. The present.

The floor is divided in four horizontal planes. Downstage is the livingroom, which is about ten feet deep. Center stage, eighteen inches high, is the diningroom, which is about ten feet deep. Further upstage, eighteen inches high, is a hallway which is about four feet deep. At each end of the hallway there is a door. The one to the right leads to the servants' quarters, the one to the left to the basement. Upstage, three feet lower than the hallway (same level as the livingroom), is the cellar, which is about sixteen feet deep. Most of the cellar is occupied by two platforms which are eight feet wide, eight feet deep, and three feet high. Upstage of the cellar are steps that lead up. Approximately ten feet above the cellar is another level, extending from the extreme left to the extreme right, which represents a warehouse. There is a door on the left of the warehouse. On the left and the right of the livingroom there are archways that lead to hallways or antechambers, the floors of these hallways are the same level as the diningroom. On the left and the right of the diningroom there is a second set of archways that lead to hallways or antechambers, the floors of which are the same level as the hallways. All along the edge of each level there is a step that leads to the next level. All floors and steps are black marble. In the livingroom there are two chairs. One is to the left, next to a table with a telephone. The other is to the right. In the diningroom there are a large green marble table and three chairs. On the cellar floor there is a mattress to the right and a chair to the left. In the warehouse there is a table and a chair to the left, and a chair and some boxes and crates to the right.

Scene 1

Orlando is doing jumping-jacks in the upper left corner of the diningroom in the dark. A light, slowly, comes up on him. He wears military breeches held by suspenders, and riding boots. He does jumping-jacks as long as it can be endured. He stops, the center area starts to become visible. There is a chair upstage of the table. There is a linen towel on the left side of the table. Orlando dries his face with the towel and sits as he puts the towel around his neck.

ORLANDO: Thirty three and I'm still a lieutenant. In two years I'll receive a promotion or I'll leave the military. I promise I will not spend time feeling sorry for myself.—Instead I will study the situation and draw an effective plan of action. I must eliminate all obstacles.—I will make the acquaintance of people in high power. If I cannot achieve this on my own merit, I will marry a woman in high circles. Leticia must not be an obstacle.—Man must have an ideal, mine is to achieve maximum power. That is my destiny.—No other interest will deter me from this. —My sexual drive is detrimental to my ideals. I must no longer be over- whelmed by sexual passion or I will be degraded beyond hope of recovery. (*Lights fade to black.*)

Scene 2

Alejo sits to the right of the diningroom table. Orlando stands to Alejo's left. He is now a lieutenant commander. He wears an army tunic, breech- es, and boots. Leticia stands to the left. She wears a dress that suggests 1940s fashion.

LETICIA: What! Me go hunting? Do you think I'm going to shoot a deer, the most beautiful animal in the world? Do you think I'm going to destroy a deer? On the contrary, I would run in the field and scream and wave my arms like a mad woman and try to scare them away so the hunters could not reach them. I'd run in front of the bullets and let the mad hunters kill me—stand in the way of the bullets—stop the bullets with my body. I don't see how anyone can shoot a deer.

ORLANDO: (*To Alejo.*) Do you understand that? You, who are her friend, can you understand that? You don't think that is madness? She's mad. Tell her that—she'll think it's you who's mad. (*To Leticia.*) Hunting is a sport! A skill! Don't talk about something you know nothing about. Must you have an opinion about every damn thing! Can't you keep your mouth shut when you don't know what you're talking about? (*Orlando exits right.*)

LETICIA: He told me that he didn't love me, and that his sole relationship to me was simply a marital one. What he means is that I am to keep this house, and he is to provide for it. That's what he said. That explains why he treats me the way he treats me. I never understood why he did, but now it's clear. He doesn't love me. I thought he loved me and that he stayed with me because he loved me and that's why I didn't understand his behavior. But now I know, because he told me that he sees me as a person who runs the house. I never understood that because I would have never—if he had said, "Would you marry me to run my house even if I don't love you." I would have never—I would have never believed what I was hearing. I would have never believed that these words were coming out of his mouth. Because I loved him. (*Orlando has entered. Leticia sees him and exits left. Orlando enters and sits center.*)

ORLANDO: I didn't say any of that. I told her that she's not my heir. That's what I said. I told her that she's not in my will, and she will not receive a penny of my money if I die. That's what I said. I didn't say anything about running the house. I said she will not inherit a penny from me because I didn't want to be humiliated. She is capable of foolishness beyond anyone's imagination. Ask her what she would do if she were rich and could do anything she wants with her money. (*Leticia enters.*)

LETICIA: I would distribute it among the poor.

ORLANDO: She has no respect for money.

LETICIA: That is not true. If I had money I would give it to those who need it. I know what money is, what money can do. It can feed people, it can put a roof over their heads. Money can do that. It can clothe them. What do you know about money? What does it mean to you? What do you do with money? Buy rifles? To shoot deer?

ORLANDO: You're foolish!—You're foolish! You're a foolish woman! (*Orlando exits. He speaks from offstage.*) Foolish. . . . Foolish. . . .

LETICIA: He has no respect for me. He is insensitive. He doesn't listen. You cannot reach him. He is deaf. He is an animal. Nothing touches him except sensuality. He responds to food, to the flesh. To music sometimes, if it is romantic. To the moon. He is romantic but he is not aware of what you are feeling. I can't change him.—I'll tell you why I asked you to come. Because I want something from you.—I want you to educate me. I want to study. I want to study so I am not an ignorant person. I want to go to the university. I want to be knowledgeable. I'm tired of being ignored. I want to study political science. Is political science what diplomats study? Is that what it is? You have to teach me elemental things because I never finished grammar school. I would have to study a great deal. A great deal so I could enter the university. I would have to go through all the subjects. I would like to be a woman who speaks in a group and have others listen.

ALEJO: Why do you want to worry about any of that? What's the use? Do you think you can change anything? Do think anyone can change anything?

LETICIA: Why not? (*Pause.*) Do you think I'm crazy?—He can't help it.—Do you think I'm crazy?—Because I love him? (*He looks away from her. Lights fade to black.*)

Scene 3

Orlando enters the warehouse holding Nena close to him. She wears a gray over-large uniform. She is barefoot. She resists him. She is tearful and frightened. She pulls away and runs to the right wall. He follows her.

ORLANDO: (*Softly.*) You called me a snake.

NENA: No, I didn't. (*He tries to reach her. She pushes his hands away from her.*) I was kidding.—I swear I was kidding.

(*He grabs her and pushes her against the wall. He pushes his pelvis against her. He moves to the chair dragging her with him. She crawls to the left, pushes the table aside and stands behind it. He walks around the table. She goes under it. He grabs her foot and pulls her out toward the downstage side. He opens his fly and pushes his pelvis against her. Lights fade to black.*)

Scene 4

Olimpia is wiping crumbs off the diningroom table. She wears a plain gray uniform. Leticia sits to the left of the table facing front. She wears a dressing gown. She writes in a notebook. There is some silverware on the table. Olimpia has a speech defect.

LETICIA: Let's do this.

OLIMPIA: O.K. (*She continues wiping the table.*)

LETICIA: (*Still writing.*) What are you doing?

OLIMPIA: I'm doing what I always do.

LETICIA: Let's do this.

OLIMPIA: (*In a mumble.*) As soon as I finish doing this. You can't just ask me to do what you want me to do, and interrupt what I'm doing. I don't stop from the time I wake up in the morning to the time I go to sleep. You can't interrupt me whenever you want, not if you want me to get to the end of my work. I wake up at 5:30. I wash. I put on my clothes and make my bed. I go to the kitchen. I get the milk and the bread from outside and I put them on the counter. I open the icebox. I put one bottle in and take the butter out. I leave the other bottle on the counter. I shut the refrigerator door. I take the pan that I use for water and put water in it. I know how much. I put the pan on the stove, light the stove, cover it. I take the top off the milk and pour it in the milk pan except for a little. (*Indicating with her finger.*) Like this. For the cat. I put the pan on the stove, light the stove. I put coffee in the thing. I know how much. I light the oven and put bread in it. I come here, get the tablecloth and I lay it on the table. I shout "Breakfast." I get the napkins. I take the cups, the saucers, and the silver out and set the table. I go to the kitchen. I put the tray on the counter, put the butter on the tray. The water and the milk are getting hot. I pick up the cat's dish. I wash it. I pour the milk I left in the bottle in the milk dish. I put it on the floor for the cat. I shout "Breakfast." The water boils. I pour it in the thing. When the milk boils I turn off the gas and cover the milk. I get the bread from the oven. I slice it down the middle and butter it. Then I cut it in pieces (*indicating*) this big. I set a piece aside for me. I put the rest of the bread in the bread dish and shout "Breakfast." I pour the coffee in the coffee pot and the milk in the milk pitcher, except I leave (*indicating*) this much for me. I put them on the tray and bring them here. If you're not in the diningroom I call again. "Breakfast." I go to the kitchen, I fill the milk pan with water and let it soak. I pour my coffee, sit at the counter and eat my breakfast. I go upstairs to make your bed and clean your bathroom. I come down here to meet you and figure out what you want for lunch and dinner. And try to get you to think quickly so I can run to the market and get it bought before all the fresh stuff is bought up. Then, I start the day.

LETICIA: So?

OLIMPIA: So I need a steam pot.

LETICIA: What is a steam pot?

OLIMPIA: A pressure cooker.

LETICIA: And you want a steam pot? Don't you have enough pots?

OLIMPIA: No.

LETICIA: Why do you want a steam pot?

OLIMPIA: It cooks faster.

LETICIA: How much is it?

OLIMPIA: Expensive.

LETICIA: How much?

OLIMPIA: Twenty.

LETICIA: Too expensive. (*Olimpia throws the silver on the floor. Leticia turns her eyes up to the ceiling.*) Why do you want one more pot?

OLIMPIA: I don't have a steam pot.

LETICIA: A pressure cooker.

OLIMPIA: A pressure cooker.

LETICIA: You have too many pots. (*Olimpia goes to the kitchen and returns with an aluminum pan. She shows it to Leticia.*)

OLIMPIA: Look at this. (*Leticia looks at it.*)

LETICIA: What? (*Olimpia hits the pan against the back of a chair, breaking off a piece of the bottom.*)

OLIMPIA: It's no good.

LETICIA: All right! (*She takes money from her pocket and gives it to Olimpia.*) Here. Buy it!—What are we having for lunch?

OLIMPIA: Fish.

LETICIA: I don't like fish.—What else?

OLIMPIA: Boiled plantains.

LETICIA: Make something I like.

OLIMPIA: Avocados. (*Leticia gives a look of resentment to Olimpia.*)

LETICIA: Why can't you make something I like?

OLIMPIA: Avocados.

LETICIA: Something that needs cooking.

OLIMPIA: Bread pudding.

LETICIA: And for dinner?

OLIMPIA: Pot roast.

LETICIA: What else?

OLIMPIA: Rice.

LETICIA: What else?

OLIMPIA: Salad.

LETICIA: What kind?

OLIMPIA: Avocado.

LETICIA: Again. (*Olimpia looks at Leticia.*)

OLIMPIA: You like avocados.

LETICIA: Not again.—Tomatoes. (*Olimpia mumbles.*) What's wrong with tomatoes besides that you don't like them? (*Olimpia mumbles.*)

Get some. (*Olimpia mumbles.*) What does that mean? (*Olimpia doesn't answer.*) Buy tomatoes.—What else?
OLIMPIA: That's all.
LETICIA: We need a green.
OLIMPIA: Watercress.
LETICIA: What else?
OLIMPIA: Nothing.
LETICIA: For dessert.
OLIMPIA: Bread pudding.
LETICIA: Again.
OLIMPIA: Why not?
LETICIA: Make a flan.
OLIMPIA: No flan.
LETICIA: Why not?
OLIMPIA: No good.
LETICIA: Why no good!—Buy some fruit then.
OLIMPIA: What kind?
LETICIA: Pineapple. (*Olimpia shakes her head.*) Why not? (*Olimpia shakes her head.*) Mango.
OLIMPIA: No mango.
LETICIA: Buy some fruit! That's all. Don't forget bread. (*Leticia hands Olimpia some bills. Olimpia holds it and waits for more. Leticia hands her one more bill. Lights fade to black.*)

Scene 5

The warehouse table is propped against the door. The chair on the left faces right. The door is pushed and the table falls to the floor. Orlando enters. He wears an undershirt with short sleeves, breeches with suspenders and boots. He looks around the room for Nena. Believing she has escaped, he becomes still and downcast. He turns to the door and stands there for a moment. He takes a few steps to the right and stands there for a moment staring fixedly. He hears a sound from behind the boxes, walks to them and takes a box off. Nena is there. Her head is covered with a blanket. He pulls the blanket off. Nena is motionless and staring into space. He looks at her for a while, then walks to the chair and sits facing right staring into space. A few moments pass. Lights fade to black.

Scene 6

Leticia speaks on the telephone to Mona.

LETICIA: Since they moved him to the new department he's different. (*Brief pause.*) He's distracted. I don't know where he goes in his mind. He doesn't listen to me. He worries. When I talk to him he doesn't listen. He's thinking about the job. He says he worries. What is there to worry about? Do you think there is anything to worry about? (*Brief pause.*) What meeting? (*Brief pause.*) Oh, sure. When is it? (*Brief pause.*) At what time? What do you mean I knew? No one told me.—I don't remember. Would you pick me up? (*Brief pause.*) At one? Isn't one early? (*Brief pause.*) Orlando may still be home at one. Sometimes he's here a little longer than usual. After lunch he sits and smokes. Don't you think one thirty will give us enough time? (*Brief pause.*) No. I can't leave while he's smoking . . . I'd rather not. I'd rather wait till he leaves. (*Brief pause.*) . . . One thirty, then. Thank you, Mona. (*Brief pause.*) See you then. Bye. (*Leticia puts down the receiver and walks to stage right area. Orlando's voice is heard offstage left. He and Alejo enter halfway through the following speech.*)

ORLANDO: He made loud sounds not high-pitched like a horse. He sounded like a whale, like a wounded whale. He was pouring liquid from everywhere, his mouth, his nose, his eyes. He was not a horse but a sexual organ.—Helpless. A viscera.—Screaming. Making strange sounds. He collapsed on top of her. She wanted him off but he collapsed on top of her and stayed there on top of her. Like gum. He looked more like a whale than a horse. A seal. His muscles were soft. What does it feel like to be without shape like that. Without pride. She was indifferent. He stayed there for a while and then lifted himself off her and to the ground. (*Pause.*) He looked like a horse again.

LETICIA: Alejo, how are you? (*Alejo kisses Leticia's hand.*)

ORLANDO: (*As he walks to the livingroom. He sits left facing front.*) Alejo is staying for dinner.

LETICIA: Would you like some coffee?

ALEJO: Yes, thank you.

LETICIA: Would you like some coffee, Orlando?

ORLANDO: Yes, thank you.

LETICIA: (*In a loud voice towards the kitchen.*) Olimpia . . .

OLIMPIA: What?

LETICIA: Coffee . . . (*Leticia sits to the right of the table. Alejo sits center.*)

ALEJO: Have you heard?

LETICIA: Yes, he's dead and I'm glad he's dead. An evil man. I knew he'd be killed. Who killed him?

ALEJO: Someone who knew him.

LETICIA: What is there to gain? So he's murdered. Someone else will do the job. Nothing will change. To destroy them all is to say we destroy us all.

ALEJO: Do you think we're all rotten?

LETICIA: Yes.

ORLANDO: A bad germ?

LETICIA: Yes.

ORLANDO: In our hearts?

LETICIA: Yes.—In our eyes.

ORLANDO: You're silly.

LETICIA: We're blind. We can't see beyond an arm's reach. We don't believe our life will last beyond the day. We only know what we have in our hand to put in our mouth, to put in our stomach, and to put in our pocket. We take care of our pocket, but not of our country. We take care of our stomachs but not of our hungry. We are primitive. We don't believe in the future. Each night when the sun goes down we think that's the end of life—so we have one last fling. We don't think we have a future. We don't think we have a country. Ask anybody, "Do you have a country?" They'll say, "Yes." Ask them, "What is your country?" They'll say, "My bed, my dinner plate." But, things can change. They can. I have changed. You have changed. He has changed.

ALEJO: Look at me. I used to be an idealist. Now I don't have any feeling for anything. I used to be strong, healthy, I looked at the future with hope.

LETICIA: Now you don't?

ALEJO: Now I don't. I know what viciousness is.

ORLANDO: What is viciousness?

ALEJO: You.

ORLANDO: Me?

ALEJO: The way you tortured Felo.

ORLANDO: I never tortured Felo.

ALEJO: You did.

ORLANDO: Boys play that way. You did too.

ALEJO: I didn't.

ORLANDO: He was repulsive to us.

ALEJO: I never hurt him.

ORLANDO: Well, you never stopped me.

ALEJO: I didn't know how to stop you. I didn't know anyone could behave the way you did. It frightened me. It changed me. I became hopeless. (*Orlando walks to the diningroom.*)

ORLANDO: You were always hopeless. (*He exits. Olimpia enters carrying three demi-tasse coffees on a tray. She places them on the table and exits.*)

ALEJO: I am sexually impotent. I have no feelings. Things pass through me which resemble feelings but I know they are not. I'm impotent.

LETICIA: Nonsense.

ALEJO: It's not nonsense. How can you say it's nonsense?—How can one live in a world that festers the way ours does and take any pleasure in life? (*Lights fade to black.*)

Scene 7

Nena and Orlando stand against the wall in the warehouse. She is fully dressed. He is barebreasted. He pushes his pelvis against her gently. His lips touch her face as he speaks. The words are inaudible to the audience. On the table there is a tin plate with food and a tin cup with milk.

ORLANDO: Look this way. I'm going to do something to you. (*She makes a move away from him.*) Don't do that. Don't move away. (*As he slides his hand along her side.*) I just want to put my hand here like this. (*He puts his lips on hers softly and speaks at the same time.*) Don't hold your lips so tight. Make them soft. Let them loose. So I can do this. (*She whimpers.*) Don't cry. I won't hurt you. This is all I'm going to do to you. Just hold your lips soft. Be nice. Be a nice girl. (*He pushes against her and reaches an orgasm. He remains motionless for a moment, then steps away from her still leaning his hand on the wall.*) Go eat. I brought you food. (*She goes to the table. He sits on the floor and watches her eat. She eats voraciously. She looks at the milk.*) Drink it. It's milk. It's good for you. (*She drinks the milk, then continues eating. Lights fade to black.*)

Scene 8

Leticia stands left of the diningroom table. She speaks words she has memorized. Olimpia sits to the left of the table. She holds a book close to her eyes. Her head moves from left to right along the written words as she mumbles the sound of imaginary words. She continues doing this through the rest of the scene.

LETICIA: The impact of war is felt particularly in the economic realm. The destruction of property, private as well as public may paralyze the country. Foreign investment is virtually . . . (*To Olimpia.*) Is that right? (*Pause.*) Is that right!

OLIMPIA: Wait a moment. (*She continues mumbling and moving her head.*)

LETICIA: What for? (*Pause.*) You can't read. (*Pause.*) You can't read!

OLIMPIA: Wait a moment. (*She continues mumbling and moving her head.*)

LETICIA: (*Slapping the book off Olimpia's hand.*) Why are you pretending you can read? (*Olimpia slaps Leticia's hands. They slap each other's hands. Lights fade to black.*)

Scene 9

Orlando sits in the livingroom. He smokes. He faces front and is thoughtful. Leticia and Olimpia are in the diningroom. Leticia wears a hat and jacket. She tries to put a leather strap through the loops of a suitcase. There is a smaller piece of luggage on the floor.

LETICIA: This strap is too wide. It doesn't fit through the loop. (*Orlando doesn't reply.*) Is this the right strap? Is this the strap that came with this suitcase? Did the strap that came with the suitcase break? If so, where is it? And when did it break? Why doesn't this strap fit the suitcase and how did it get here. Did you buy this strap, Orlando?

ORLANDO: I may have.

LETICIA: It doesn't fit.

ORLANDO: Hm.

LETICIA: It doesn't fit through the loops.

ORLANDO: Just strap it outside the loops. (*Leticia stands. Olimpia tries to put the strap through the loop.*)

LETICIA: No. You're supposed to put it through the loops. That's what the loops are for. What happened to the other strap?

ORLANDO: It broke.

LETICIA: How?

ORLANDO: I used it for something.

LETICIA: What! (*He looks at her.*) You should have gotten me one that fit. What did you use it for?—Look at that.

ORLANDO: Strap it outside the loops.

LETICIA: That wouldn't look right.

ORLANDO: (*Going to look at the suitcase.*) Why do you need the straps?

LETICIA: Because they come with it.

ORLANDO: You don't need them.

LETICIA: And travel like this?

ORLANDO: Use another suitcase.

LETICIA: What other suitcase. I don't have another. (*Orlando looks at his watch.*)

ORLANDO: You're going to miss your plane.

LETICIA: I'm not going. I'm not travelling like this.

ORLANDO: Go without it. I'll send it to you.

LETICIA: You'll get new luggage, repack it and send it to me?—All right. (*She starts to exit left.*) It's nice to travel light. (*Off stage.*) Do I have everything?—Come, Olimpia.

(*Olimpia follows with the suitcases. Orlando takes the larger suitcase from Olimpia. She exits. Orlando goes up the hallway and exits through the left door. A moment later he enters holding Nena close to him. She is pale, dishevelled and has black circles around her eyes. She has a high fever and is almost unconscious. Her dress is torn and soiled. She is barefoot. He carries a new cotton dress on his arm. He takes her to the chair in the livingroom. He takes off the soiled dress and puts the new dress on her over a soiled slip.*)

ORLANDO: That's nice. You look nice. (*Leticia's voice is heard. He hurriedly takes Nena out the door, closes it, and leans on it.*)
LETICIA: (*Off stage.*) It would take but a second. You run to the garage and get the little suitcase and I'll take out the things I need. (*Leticia and Olimpia enter left. Olimpia exits right.*) Hurry. Hurry. It would take but a second. (*Seeing Orlando.*) Orlando, I came back because I couldn't leave without anything at all. I came to get a few things because I have a smaller suitcase where I can take a few things. (*She puts the suitcase on the table, opens it and takes out the things she mentions.*) A pair of shoes . . . (*Olimpia enters right with a small suitcase.*)
OLIMPIA: Here.

LETICIA:	OLIMPIA:
A nightgown,	A robe,
a robe,	a dress,
underwear,	a nightgown,
a dress,	underwear,
a sweater.	a sweater,
	a pair of shoes.

(*Leticia closes the large suitcase. Olimpia closes the smaller suitcase.*)

LETICIA: (*Starting to exit.*) Goodbye.
OLIMPIA: (*Following Leticia.*) Goodbye.
ORLANDO: Goodbye. (*Lights fade to black.*)

Scene 10

Nena is curled on the extreme right of the mattress. Orlando sits on the mattress using Nena as a back support. Alejo sits on the chair. He holds a green paper on his hand. Olimpia sweeps the floor.

ORLANDO: Tell them to check him. See if there's a scratch on him. There's not a scratch on that body. Why the fuss! Who was he and who's making a fuss? Why is he so important.

ALEJO: He was in deep. He knew names.

ORLANDO: I was never told that. But it wouldn't have mattered if they had because he died before I touched him.

ALEJO: You have to go to headquarters. They want you there.

ORLANDO: He came in screaming and he wouldn't stop. I had to wait for him to stop screaming before I could even pose a question to him. He wouldn't stop. I had put the poker to his neck to see if he would stop. Just to see if he would shut up. He just opened his eyes wide and started shaking and screamed even louder and fell over dead. Maybe he took something. I didn't do anything to him. If I didn't get anything from him it's because he died before I could get to him. He died of fear, not from anything I did to him. Tell them to do an autopsy. I'm telling you the truth. That's the truth. Why the fuss.

ALEJO: (*Starting to put the paper in his pocket.*) I'll tell them what you said.

ORLANDO: Let me see that. (*Alejo takes it to him. Orlando looks at it and puts it back in Alejo's hands.*) O.K. so it's a trap. So what side are you on? (*Pause. Alejo says nothing.*) So what do they want? (*Pause.*) Who's going to question me? That's funny. That's very funny. They want to question me. They want to punch my eyes out? I knew something was wrong because they were getting nervous. Antonio was getting nervous. I went to him and I asked him if something was wrong. He said, no, nothing was wrong. But I could tell something was wrong. He looked at Velez and Velez looked back at him. They are stupid. They want to conceal something from me and they look at each other right in front of me, as if I'm blind, as if I can't tell that they are worried about something. As if there's something happening right in front of my nose but I'm blind and I can't see it. (*He grabs the paper from Alejo's hand.*) You understand? (*He goes up the steps.*)

OLIMPIA: Like an alligator, big mouth and no brains. Lots of teeth but no brains. All tongue. (*Orlando enters through the left hallway door, and sits at the diningroom table. Alejo enters a few moments later. He stands to the right.*)

ORLANDO: What kind of way is this to treat me?—After what I've done for them?—Is this a way to treat me?—I'll come up . . . as soon as I can—I haven't been well.—O.K. I'll come up. I get depressed because things are bad and they are not going to improve. There's something malignant in the world. Destructiveness, aggressiveness.—Greed. People take what is not theirs. There is greed. I am depressed, disillusioned . . . with life . . . with work . . . family. I don't see hope. (*He sits. He speaks more to himself than to Alejo.*) Some people get a cut in a finger and die. Because their veins are right next to their skin. There are people who, if you punch them in their stomach the skin around the stomach bursts and the bowels fall out. Other people, you cut them open and you don't see any veins. You can't find their intestines. There are people who don't even bleed. There are people who bleed like pigs. There are people who have the nerves right on their skins. You touch them and they scream. They have their vital organs close to the surface. You hit them and they burst an organ. I didn't even touch this one and he died. He died of fear. (*Lights fade to black.*)

Scene 11

Nena, Alejo and Olimpia sit cross-legged on the mattress in the basement. Nena sits right, Alejo center, Olimpia left. Nena and Olimpia play patty-cake. Orlando enters. He goes close to them.

ORLANDO: What are you doing?

OLIMPIA: I'm playing with her.

ORLANDO: (*To Alejo.*) What are you doing here? (*Alejo looks at Orlando as a reply. Orlando speaks sarcastically.*) They're playing pattycake. (*He goes near Nena.*) So? (*Short pause. Nena giggles.*) Stop laughing! (*Nena is frightened. Olimpia holds her.*)

OLIMPIA: Why do you have to spoil everything. We were having a good time.

ORLANDO: Shut up! (*Nena whimpers.*) Stop whimpering. I can't stand your whimpering. I can't stand it. (*Timidly, she tries to speak words as she whimpers.*) Speak up. I can't hear you! She's crazy! Take her to the crazy house!

OLIMPIA: She's not crazy! She's a baby!

ORLANDO: She's not a baby! She's crazy! You think she's a baby? She's older than you think! How old do you think she is—Don't tell me that.

OLIMPIA: She's sick. Don't you see she's sick? Let her cry! (*To Nena.*) Cry!

ORLANDO: You drive me crazy too with your . . . (*He imitates her speech defect. She punches him repeatedly.*)

OLIMPIA: You drive me crazy! (*He pushes her off.*) You drive me crazy! You are a bastard! One day I'm going to kill you when you're asleep! I'm going to open you up and cut your entrails and feed them to the snakes. (*She tries to strangle him.*) I'm going to tear your heart out and feed it to the dogs! I'm going to cut your head open and have the cats eat your brain! (*Reaching for his fly.*) I'm going to cut your peepee and hang it on a tree and feed it to the birds!

ORLANDO: Get off me! I'm getting rid of you too! (*He starts to exit.*) I can't stand you!

OLIMPIA: Oh, yeah! I'm getting rid of you.

ORLANDO: I can't stand you!

OLIMPIA: I can't stand you!

ORLANDO: Meddler! (*To Alejo.*) I can't stand you either.

OLIMPIA: (*Going to the stairs.*) Tell the boss! Tell her! She won't get rid of me! She'll get rid of you! What good are you! Tell her! (*She goes to Nena.*) Don't pay any attention to him. He's a coward.—You're pretty. (*Orlando enters through the hallway left door. He sits center at the diningroom table and leans his head on it. Leticia enters. He turns to look at her.*)

LETICIA: You didn't send it. (*Lights fade to black.*)

Scene 12

Leticia sits next to the phone. She speaks to Mona in her mind.

LETICIA: I walk through the house and I know where he's made love to her I think I hear his voice making love to her. Saying the same things he says to me, the same words.— (*There is a pause.*) There is someone here. He keeps someone here in the house. (*Pause.*) I don't dare look. (*Pause.*) No, there's nothing I can do. I can't do anything. (*She walks to the hallway. She hears footsteps. She moves rapidly to left and hides behind a pillar. Olimpia enters from right. She takes a few steps down the hallway. She carries a plate of food. She sees Leticia and stops. She takes a few steps in various directions, then stops.*)

OLIMPIA: Here kitty, kitty. (*Leticia walks to Olimpia, looks closely at the plate, then up at Olimpia.*)

LETICIA: What is it?

OLIMPIA: Food.

LETICIA: Who is it for? (*Olimpia turns her eyes away and doesn't answer. Leticia decides to go to the cellar door. She stops halfway there.*) Who is it?

OLIMPIA: A cat. (*Leticia opens the cellar door.*)

LETICIA: It's not a cat. I'm going down. (*She opens the door to the cellar and starts to go down.*) I want to see who is there.

ORLANDO: (*Offstage from the cellar.*) What is it you want? (*Lights fade to black.*)

Scene 13

Orlando leans back on the chair in the basement. His legs are outstretched. His eyes are bloodshot and leery. His tunic is open. Nena is curled on the floor. Orlando speaks quietly. He is deeply absorbed.

ORLANDO: What I do to you is out of love. Out of want. It's not what you think. I wish you didn't have to be hurt. I don't do it out of hatred. It is not out of rage. It is love. It is a quiet feeling. It's a pleasure. It is quiet and it pierces my insides in the most internal way. It is my most private self. And this I give to you.—Don't be afraid.—It is a desire to destroy and to see things destroyed and to see the inside of them.—It's my nature. I must hide this from others. But I don't feel remorse. I was born this way and I must have this.—I need love. I wish you did not feel hurt and recoil from me. (*Lights fade to black.*)

Scene 14

Orlando sits to the right and Leticia sits to the left of the table.

LETICIA: Don't make her scream. (*There is a pause.*)
ORLANDO: You're crazy.
LETICIA: Don't I give you enough?
ORLANDO: (*He's calm.*) Don't start.
LETICIA: How long is she going to be here?
ORLANDO: Not long.
LETICIA: Don't make her cry. (*He looks at her.*) I can't stand it. (*Pause.*) Why do you make her scream?
ORLANDO: I don't make her scream.
LETICIA: She screams.
ORLANDO: I can't help it. (*Pause.*)
LETICIA: I tell you I can't stand it. I'm going to ask Mona to come and stay with me.
ORLANDO: No.
LETICIA: I want someone here with me.
ORLANDO: I don't want her here.
LETICIA: Why not?
ORLANDO: I don't.
LETICIA: I need someone here with me.
ORLANDO: Not now.
LETICIA: When?
ORLANDO: Soon enough.—She's going to stay here for a while. She's going to work for us. She'll be a servant here.

LETICIA: . . . No.

ORLANDO: She's going to be a servant here. (*Lights fade to black.*)

Scene 15

Olimpia and Nena are sitting at the diningroom table. They are separating stones and other matter from dry beans.

NENA: I used to clean beans when I was in the home. And also string beans. I also pressed clothes. The days were long. Some girls did hand sewing. They spent the day doing that. I didn't like it. When I did that, the day was even longer and there were times when I couldn't move even if I tried. And they said I couldn't go there anymore, that I had to stay in the yard. I didn't mind sitting in the yard looking at the birds. I went to the laundryroom and watched the women work. They let me go in and sit there. And they showed me how to press. I like to press because my mind wanders and I find satisfaction. I can iron all day. I like the way the wrinkles come out and things look nice. It's a miracle isn't it? I could earn a living pressing clothes. And I could find my grandpa and take care of him.

OLIMPIA: Where is your grandpa?

NENA: I don't know. (*They work a little in silence.*) He sleeps in the streets. Because he's too old to remember where he lives. He needs a person to take care of him. And I can take care of him. But I don't know where he is.—He doesn't know where I am.—He doesn't know who he is. He's too old. He doesn't know anything about himself. He only knows how to beg. And he knows that, only because he's hungry. He walks around and begs for food. He forgets to go home. He lives in the camp for the homeless and he has his own box. It's not an ugly box like the others. It is a real box. I used to live there with him. He took me with him when my mother died till they took me to the home. It is a big box. It's big enough for two. I could sleep in the front where it's cold. And he could sleep in the back where it's warmer. And he could lean on me. The floor is hard for him because he's skinny and it's hard on his poor bones. He could sleep on top of me if that would make him feel comfortable. I wouldn't mind. Except that he may pee on me because he pees in his pants. He doesn't know not to. He is incontinent. He can't hold it. His box was a little smelly. But that doesn't matter because I could clean it. All I would need is some soap. I could get plenty of water from the public faucet. And I could borrow a brush. You know how clean I could get it? As clean as new. You know what I would do? I would make holes in the floor so the pee would go down to the ground. And you know what else I would do?

OLIMPIA: What?

NENA: I would get straw and put it on the floor for him and for me and it would make it comfortable and clean and warm. How do you like that? Just as I did for my goat.

OLIMPIA: You have a goat?

NENA: . . . I did.

OLIMPIA: What happened to him?

NENA: He died. They killed him and ate him. Just like they did Christ.

OLIMPIA: Nobody ate Christ.

NENA: . . . I thought they did. My goat was eaten though.—In the home we had clean sheets. But that doesn't help. You can't sleep on clean sheets, not if there isn't someone watching over you while you sleep. And since my ma died there just wasn't anyone watching over me. Except you.—Aren't you? In the home they said guardian angels watch your sleep, but I didn't see any there. There weren't any. One day I heard my grandpa calling me and I went to look for him. And I didn't find him. I got tired and I slept in the street, and I was hungry and I was crying. And then he came to me and he spoke to me very softly so as not to scare me and he said he would give me something to eat and he said he would help me look for my grandpa. And he put me in the back of his van . . . And he took me to a place. And he hurt me. I fought with him but I stopped fighting—because I couldn't fight anymore and he did things to me. And he locked me in. And sometimes he brought me food and sometimes he didn't. And he did things to me. And he beat me. And he hung me on the wall. And I got sick. And sometimes he brought me medicine. And then he said he had to take me somewhere. And he brought me here. And I am glad to be here because you are here. I only wish my grandpa were here too. He doesn't beat me so much anymore.

OLIMPIA: Why does he beat you? I hear him at night. He goes down the steps and I hear you cry. Why does he beat you?

NENA: Because I'm dirty.

OLIMPIA: You are not dirty.

NENA: I am. That's why he beats me. The dirt won't go away from inside me.—He comes downstairs when I'm sleeping and I hear him coming and it frightens me. And he takes the covers off me and I don't move because I'm frightened and because I feel cold and I think I'm going to die. And he puts his hand on me and he recites poetry. And he is almost naked. He wears a robe but he leaves it open and he feels himself as he recites. He touches himself and he touches his stomach and his breasts and his behind. He puts his fingers in my parts and he keeps reciting. Then he turns me on my stomach and puts himself inside me. And he says I belong to him. (*There is a pause.*) I want to conduct each day of my life in the best possible way. I should value the things I have. And I should value all those who are near me. And I should value the kindness that others bestow upon me. And if someone should treat me unkindly, I should not blind myself with rage, but I should see them and receive them, since maybe they are in worse pain than me. (*Lights fade to black.*)

Scene 16

Leticia speaks on the telephone with Mona. She speaks rapidly.

LETICIA: He is violent. He has become more so. I sense it. I feel it in him. —I understand his thoughts. I know what he thinks.—I raised him. I practically did. He was a boy when I met him. I saw him grow. I was the first woman he loved. That's how young he was. I have to look after him, make sure he doesn't get into trouble. He's not wise. He's trusting. They are changing him.—He tortures people. I know he does. He tells me he doesn't but I know he does. I know it. How could I not. Sometimes he comes from headquarters and his hands are shaking. Why should he shake? What do they do there?—He should transfer. Why do that? He says he doesn't do it himself. That the officers don't do it. He says that people are not being tortured. That that is questionable.—Everybody knows it. How could he not know it when everybody knows it. Sometimes you see blood in the streets. Haven't you seen it? Why do they leave the bodies in the streets,—how evil, to frighten people? They tear their fingernails off and their poor hands are bloody and destroyed. And they mangle their genitals and expose them and they tear their eyes out and you can see the empty eyesockets in the skull. How awful, Mona. He musn't do it. I don't care if I don't have anything! What's money! I don't need a house as big as this! He's doing it for money! What other reason could he have! What other reason could he have!! He shouldn't do it. I cannot look at him without thinking of it. He's doing it. I know he's doing it.—Shhhh! I hear steps. I'll call you later. Bye, Mona. I'll talk to you. (*She hangs up the receiver. Lights fade to black.*)

Scene 17

The livingroom. Olimpia sits to the right, Nena to the left.

OLIMPIA: I don't wear high heels because they hurt my feet. I used to have a pair but they hurt my feet and also (*Pointing to her calf.*) here in my legs. So I don't wear them anymore even if they were pretty. Did you ever wear high heels? (*Nena shakes her head.*) Do you have ingrown nails? (*Nena looks at her questioningly.*) Nails that grow twisted into the flesh. (*Nena shakes her head.*) I don't either. Do you have sugar in the blood? (*Nena shakes her head.*) My mother had sugar in the blood and that's what she died of but she lived to be eighty six which is very old even if she had many things wrong with her. She had glaucoma and high blood pressure. (*Leticia enters and sits center at the table. Nena starts to get up. Olimpia signals her to be still. Leticia is not concerned with them.*)

LETICIA: So, what are you talking about?

OLIMPIA: Ingrown nails. (*Nena turns to Leticia to make sure she may remain seated there. Leticia is involved with her own thoughts. Nena turns front. Lights fade to black.*)

Scene 18

Orlando is sleeping on the diningroom table. The telephone rings. He speaks as someone having a nightmare.

ORLANDO: Ah! Ah! Ah! Get off me! Get off! I said get off! (*Leticia enters.*)

LETICIA: (*Going to him.*) Orlando! What's the matter! What are you doing here!

ORLANDO: Get off me! Ah! Ah! Ah! Get off me!

LETICIA: Why are you sleeping here! On the table. (*Holding him close to her.*) Wake up.

ORLANDO: Let go of me. (*He slaps her hands as she tries to reach him.*) Get away from me. (*He goes to the floor on his knees and staggers to the telephone.*) Yes. Yes, it's me.—You did?—So?—It's true then.— What's the name?—Yes, sure.—Thanks.—Sure. (*He hangs up the receiver. He turns to look at Leticia. Lights fade to black.*)

Scene 19

Two chairs are placed side by side facing front in the center of the living room. Leticia sits on the right. Orlando stands on the down left corner. Nena sits to the left of the dining room table facing front. She covers her face. Olimpia stands behind her, holding Nena and leaning her head on her.

ORLANDO: Talk.

LETICIA: I can't talk like this.

ORLANDO: Why not?

LETICIA: In front of everyone.

ORLANDO: Why not?

LETICIA: It is personal. I don't need the whole world to know.

ORLANDO: Why not?

LETICIA: Because it's private. My life is private.

ORLANDO: Are you ashamed?

LETICIA: Yes, I am ashamed!

ORLANDO: What of . . . ? What of . . . ? — I want you to tell us—about your lover.

LETICIA: I don't have a lover. (*He grabs her by the hair. Olimpia holds on to Nena and hides her face. Nena covers her face.*)

ORLANDO: You have a lover.

LETICIA: That's a lie.

ORLANDO: (*Moving closer to her.*) It's not a lie. (*To Leticia.*) Come on tell us. (*He pulls harder.*) What's his name? (*She emits a sound of pain. He pulls harder, leans toward her and speaks in a low tone.*) What's his name?

LETICIA: Albertico. (*He takes a moment to release her.*)

ORLANDO: Tell us about it. (*There is silence. He pulls her hair.*)

LETICIA: All right. (*He releases her.*)

ORLANDO: What's his name?

LETICIA: Albertico.

ORLANDO: Go on. (*Pause.*) Sit up! (*She does.*) Albertico what?

LETICIA: Estevez. (*Orlando sits next to her.*)

ORLANDO: Go on. (*Silence.*) Where did you first meet him?

LETICIA: At . . . I . . .

ORLANDO: (*He grabs her by the hair.*) In my office.

LETICIA: Yes.

ORLANDO: Don't lie. —When?

LETICIA: You know when.

ORLANDO: When! (*Silence.*) How did you meet him?

LETICIA: You introduced him to me. (*He lets her go.*)

ORLANDO: What else? (*Silence.*) Who is he!

LETICIA: He's a lieutenant.

ORLANDO: (*He stands.*) When did you meet with him?

LETICIA: Last week.

ORLANDO: When!

LETICIA: Last week.

ORLANDO: When!

LETICIA: Last week. I said last week.

ORLANDO: Where did you meet him?

LETICIA: . . . In a house of rendez-vous . . .

ORLANDO: How did you arrange it?
LETICIA: . . . I wrote to him . . . !
ORLANDO: Did he approach you?
LETICIA: No.
ORLANDO: Did he!
LETICIA: No.
ORLANDO: (*He grabs her hair again.*) He did! How!
LETICIA: *I* approached him.
ORLANDO: How!
LETICIA: (*Aggressively.*) I looked at him! I looked at him! I looked at him!
   (*He lets her go.*)
ORLANDO: When did you look at him?
LETICIA: Please stop . . . !
ORLANDO: Where! When!
LETICIA: In your office!
ORLANDO: When?
LETICIA: I asked him to meet me!
ORLANDO: What did he say?
LETICIA: (*Aggressively.*) He walked away. He walked away! He walked
   away! I asked him to meet me.
ORLANDO: What was he like?
LETICIA: . . . Oh . . .
ORLANDO: Was he tender? Was he tender to you!

(*She doesn't answer. He puts his hand inside her blouse. She lets out an ex-
crutiating scream. He lets her go and walks to the right of the diningroom. She goes to the telephone table, opens the drawer, takes a gun
and shoots Orlando. Orlando falls dead. Nena runs to downstage of the
table. Leticia is disconcerted, then puts the revolver in Nena's hand and
steps away from her.*)

LETICIA: Please . . .

(*Nena is in a state of terror and numb acceptance. She looks at the gun.
Then, up. The lights fade.*)

END

Sarita

Sarita was first produced at INTAR, 420 West 42nd Street, New York City, on January 18, 1984. Music was composed by Leon Odenz. The play was directed by the author with the following cast:

Yeye	Blanca Camacho
Sarita	Sheila Dabney
Fela	Carmen Rosario
Fernando	Rodolfo Diaz
Julio	Michael Carmine
Mark	Tom Kirk
Juan	Bambu

Sets: Donald Eastman
Lights: Anne E. Militello
Costumes: Gabriel Berry

CHARACTERS:

Sarita: A spirited young woman; age range: 13-21.
Yeye: Her friend and neighbor; age range: 13-21.
Fela: Her mother; age range: 35-43.
Fernando: Fela's tenant; age range: 60-68.
Julio: Sarita's lover; age range: 15-23.
Mark: Sarita's husband; age range: 20-24.
Juan: A friend and drummer.

The set represents Fela's livingroom in New York's South Bronx. However, the proportions are not realistic. The ceiling is inordinately high. There are no windows except for a small one, ten feet high on each side wall. There are two doors in the back wall. In the livingroom there are an overstuffed couch, two overstuffed chairs, a coffee table, and two footstools on each side of the coffee table. The orchestra pit is behind the back wall. Seven feet above is an open recess or a rectangular cut-out on the back wall which is Sarita's kitchen. There is a kitchen table and two chairs. To the left on the livingroom back wall there is a window. There are three backdrops which are lowered in the course of the play. They are: the upper floors of the Empire State Building, a beach and the waitingroom of a mental hospital.

LIST OF SCENES:

Scene	Title	Year
ACT I		
1	Fortune Telling	1939
2	I'm Pregnant	1940
3	Conference	1940 (a few days later)
4	Fela's Song	1940
5	Sarita Leaves	1942
6	The Mirror	1942 (the next day)
7	1st Letter	1943
8	2nd Letter	1943 (six months later)
9	3rd Letter	1944
10	Empire State	1944 (a few hours later)
ACT II		
11	The Party	1944 (two months later)
12	The Letter	1945
13	Summer Resort	1945 (six months later)
14	Prayer	1945 (a few days later)
15	I Don't Love You	1946
16	By the Window	1946 (a few days later)
17	The Key	1947
18	Drinking	1947 (a few hours later)
19	Death Scene	1947 (three months later)
20	Mental Hospital	1947 (three months later)

ACT ONE

Scene 1
1939—Fortune Telling

Fela's livingroom. Sarita is 13 years old. She sits to the right of the table. Yeye sits to the left. They both wear parochial school uniforms. Yeye holds a deck of cards. She speaks rapidly as she puts the cards down.

YEYE: 1- merengue. 2- big love. 3- rice pudding. 4- sticks. 5- butterfly. 6- everything. 7- beauty. 8- pork rind. 9- things. 10- string beans. 11- this is you. 12- cherries. 13- poppies. 14- candy. 15- hope. 16- you're welcome. 17- snails. 18- greens. 19- the same. 20- not enough. 21- saffron. 22- teenth which is teeth. 23- roses. 24- a denture. 25- you get nothing. 26- pink dress. 27- rice and beans. 28- something happens to you. 29- a tree. 30- red bird. 31- Rita. Who is Rita?

SARITA: I don't know.

YEYE: 32- no eight. Where is eight? Here. (*Turning the eighth card face down.*) No eight. Turn it down. 33- pan pan pan, like this, (*tapping the card*) pan pan pan. 34- we're almost finished. 35- this and 20 no. (*She turns 35 and 20 down.*) 36- sailors. 37- horse's head. 38- old woman. 39- nothing. 40- don't smoke. 41- here's the old man. 42- tea. To drink. 43- lantern. What is that? It's upside down. 44- toga. What the Greek wears. 45- five. (*Looking back at 5.*) Five is butterfly. This is five. You understand?

SARITA: Hm.

YEYE: 46- onions. 47- you owe me three dollars. 48- many thongs which is things. 49- nauturally. What? 50- sickness. 51- nayts. 52- this is the last one. (*Looking back at cards 48, 49, 50, 51, 52.*) These came out upside down. This one is things. It came out thongs. Naturally, which came out nauturally. Sickness. You know what that is. Nayts is nights. And the last one is spike which is spoke. You understand? (*Sarita nods doubtfully.*) What did you want to know?

SARITA: Whether he loves me or not.

YEYE: Give me three quarters. (*Sarita gets three quarters.*) Put them here. (*Sarita places them on the table. Yeye taps the coins as she speaks.*) One, two, three. Quarter, quarter, quarter. He loves you.

SARITA: He does?

YEYE: See? This one is like this. This one's like this and this one is like this. Don't you see? What else do you want to know?

SARITA: If he loves me a lot.

YEYE: Give me three quarters. (*Sarita takes three quarters.*) Put them down. (*She does.*) One, two, three. Quarter, quarter, quarter. Yes, he loves you a lot.

SARITA: What was he doing with her?

YEYE: Give me three quarters.

SARITA: I don't have no more quarters.

YEYE: What do you have?

SARITA: Pennies.

YEYE: Give me pennies. (*Sarita puts three pennies on the table.*) One, two, three. Penny, penny, penny. He wasn't doing anything.

SARITA: I saw him do it.

YEYE: Do what?

SARITA: He was with her.

YEYE: He wasn't doing it.

SARITA: How do you know?

YEYE: It says so here.

SARITA: Where?

YEYE: I told you where.

SARITA: You didn't say anything.

YEYE: I told you plenty.

SARITA: You said nothing.

YEYE: What do you mean nothing?

SARITA: Nothing.

YEYE: Ungrateful! Say you're sorry to the cards.

SARITA: I'm sorry.

YEYE: What else do you want to know?

SARITA: If he loves me.

YEYE: I said he does.

SARITA: Where did you see it! Where? Show me! You didn't see it! You're just saying it! (*Reaching for the coins.*) Give me my money!

YEYE: Your fingers will rot. (*Sarita pulls back. Yeye takes the coins.*) What else do you want to know?

SARITA: You said he wasn't doing anything.

YEYE: He wasn't.

SARITA: Why was his thing standing up?

YEYE: What was?

SARITA: His thing.

YEYE: Was it?

SARITA: Would I lie to you? And he had his hand on it.

YEYE: He was scratching it. He had an itch.

SARITA: He didn't have an itch. He had something else. I know what he had. I know when he's hot. He was hot. Son of a bitch. I'm going to cut it off.

YEYE: No, you're not. He was just talking to her.

SARITA: Where is he! I'm going to cut it off!

YEYE: They'll put you in jail.

SARITA: Not me!

YEYE: Yes, they will!

SARITA: I'll tell them what he did!

YEYE: They won't care! They'll put you in jail!

SARITA: Let them! I'll kill them if they do!

YEYE: They'll burn you if you do.

SARITA: I'll kill him and her too!

YEYE: Who is she?

SARITA: It doesn't matter! (*She brushes some cards off the table.*)

YEYE: Pick them up or you'll rot in hell.

SARITA: (*Picking up the cards.*) Do you think he cares! Do you think he cares who she is! He doesn't care! He doesn't care who it is! He doesn't care! Anyone! That's who it is. Anyone! I'll kill him!

YEYE: (*Looks at a card.*) He was just talking to her.

SARITA: What about!

YEYE: Work.

SARITA: Whose work! He doesn't work.

YEYE: He was talking about work.

SARITA: And how come his thing was sticking up?

YEYE: He was thinking of you.

SARITA: You're lying.

YEYE: (*Pointing.*) Here it is.

SARITA: What is that?

YEYE: Sticks. (*She sings "He Was Thinking of You."*)

> He was thinking of you,
> that's what it means.
> He was thinking of you,
> not of her.

He called you.
You weren't home.
He walked up and down the block.
He called again,
you weren't there.
He turned the corner.
He paced up and down
and stopped a while.
She came along.
They started talking.
He was thinking of you,
that's what it means.
He was thinking of you,
not of her.
He didn't notice
he got aroused.
He was embarrassed
and covered himself
with his hand.

SARITA: He didn't notice. Don't tell me he didn't notice. He noticed! (*She sings "I'm Pudding."*)

I'm at school
I think of him and I
I get excited. I do.
I get excited. I do.
I think of him and I'm pudding.

I'm pudding. . . . But I wait. Why can't he wait?

YEYE: Give me a dollar.

SARITA: I'm not giving you no "dollar."

YEYE: What is his name?

SARITA: You know his name.

YEYE: You have to say it so the cards hear it.

SARITA: Julio. (*In a softer tone.*) Julio. . . .

YEYE: Boba.

SARITA: Boba tu.

YEYE: (*Holding Sarita's hands between hers in a position of prayer.*) Put your hands together.

SARITA & YEYE: (*They sing "Holy Spirit, Good Morning."*)

Holy spirit,
bring your daughter,
Sara Fernandez,
what she wants
and prays for.

Holy spirit,
don't forsake her,
give your daughter
all she prays
and asks for.

YEYE: Holy spirit, good morning.
SARITA: Good morning.
YEYE: Holy spirit, good night.
SARITA: Good night.
YEYE: Holy spirit, good day.
SARITA: Good day.
YEYE: Holy spirit, good week.
SARITA: Good week.
YEYE: Holy spirit, good month.
SARITA: Good month.
YEYE: Holy spirit, good year.
SARITA: Good year.

SARITA: Yeye, I think I'm going to die. I think I'm going to die. I think I'm dying. Tell me I'm not dying.—He takes my life with him when he leaves me.
YEYE: It's not so.
SARITA: It is. Look at me. I'm dead.
YEYE: You're not dead. (*Taking Sarita's hand and putting it over the cards.*) Put your hand here.
SARITA: I'm going to do what he does. I'm going out with every guy I meet.—I am. I'm not going to sit here and wait for him.
YEYE: He loves you, Sari.
SARITA: Like hell he does.
YEYE: Ask the cards to make him be true. (*Sarita closes her eyes tight for a moment. Then, opens them.*) Did you?
SARITA: Yes.
YEYE: (*Taking the cards.*) O.K. I'm going home now.
SARITA: Good bye, Yeye, you're good.
YEYE: Good bye, dummy. (*She drops a card. She starts to pick it up and stops. She looks at it.*)
SARITA: What is it?
YEYE: (*Picking it up.*) Nothing.

(*Yeye exits. Lights fade to black. Music is heard.*)

Scene 2
1940—I'm Pregnant

Fela's livingroom. Sarita is 14 years old. She lies on the couch. Her feet are up against the couch's back. Her head touches the floor. She has been crying. Fela enters. Sarita wears a parochial school uniform. Fela wears a house dress.

FELA: What's the matter with you?
SARITA: I'm pregnant.
FELA: Don't talk stupid.
SARITA: I'm not talking stupid. I'm pregnant.
FELA: You're a child. You can't be pregnant.
SARITA: I'm serious.
FELA: Would you sit like a normal person? (*Sarita sits up. Fela notices her tears.*) Why are you crying?
SARITA: I'm pregnant. . . .

(*There is a pause.*)

FELA: Who says?—You're a child. A baby. Who says!
SARITA: I'm pregnant. No one has to say it.
FELA: You're a kid. Not even in high school. What would your teacher say?
SARITA: My teacher. . . ? I don't care. . . .
FELA: (*Grabbing her by the arm.*) You don't care? (*She looks into her eyes.*) Are you telling the truth? You're lying! It isn't true!
SARITA: It's true.
FELA: How do you know?
SARITA: I missed my period and my breasts hurt. And I know I'm pregnant.
FELA: You're lying!
SARITA: I'm not! Stop saying that! It's true!
FELA: (*Shaking her.*) Why did you do that! To ruin your life! To spend your life on relief. Like a worm on relief, crawling with children. Is that how I raised you? Is that what I taught you? (*Slapping her.*) You embarrass me!
SARITA: Don't!
FELA: What is this! (*Slapping her.*) What is this!
SARITA: Don't, Mami!
FELA: I didn't even start watching you! (*Slapping her.*) I didn't even start!
SARITA: Don't hit me, Mami!
FELA: I didn't think I had to watch you! (*Slapping her.*) You are a kid!

(*Sarita runs left, goes around the chair and sits on it wailing.*) You're a kid! (*Raising her arms up in the air.*) I didn't even start watching you! (*Going on her knees. Her arms are raised.*) It's my fault! I didn't watch you! (*Pulling her hair and beating her chest.*) It's my fault!

SARITA: No Mami!

FELA: It's my fault!

SARITA: It's not your fault!

FELA: It's my fault! I let you loose in the street!

SARITA: No, Mami.

FELA: It's my fault! (*She starts to cry.*) It is my fault. . . . It is my fault. . . .

SARITA: Don't cry, Mami.

FELA: (*Starting to stand.*) Where's that kid! Julio!

SARITA: (*Crawls on her knees and grabs Fela.*) It wasn't him!

FELA: Where is he!

SARITA: It wasn't him!

FELA: Who was it!

SARITA: I don't know!

FELA: Somebody raped you!

SARITA: No!

FELA: Fernando raped you!

SARITA: No, he didn't!

FELA: He's a dirty old man! I knew he was!

SARITA: No!

FELA: Who gave you a baby!

SARITA: Nobody!

FELA: (*Grabbing her.*) Who did it!

SARITA: I don't know.

FELA: Tell me or I'll kill you.

SARITA: Don't make me tell you.

FELA: Tell me.

SARITA: I went out a lot.

FELA: Who with?

SARITA: With a lot of guys! I don't know who did it! I went out with a lot of guys!

FELA: You don't know who did it?

SARITA: Mami, I was crying all the time. I was unhappy. I had tears in my eyes all the time. You know how I used to be. Julio left me. I was unhappy. You can't think of anything when you're unhappy like that. I went with boys and I felt better. I didn't care who they were. I was unhappy. You know how I was, Mami. You know I get crazy when he leaves me. You know I was crazy. I didn't know what I was doing. Don't be angry, Mami. It's hard enough. . . .

FELA: (*Lowers her head.*) . . . I raised you wrong. You didn't have a father. And you didn't have a family. Just me. I didn't teach you right.
SARITA: It's not that, Mami. You taught me right. (*She holds Fela tightly.*) It's just that I don't understand. . . . I'm a savage. . . . Other people don't have to learn how to be. But I'm a savage. I have to learn how to lead my life.

(*She cries. Fela puts her arms around her. Lights fade to black. Music is heard.*)

Scene 3
1940—Conference

A few days later. Fela's livingroom. Fernando sits on the couch. Fela sits to the left. Sarita sits to the right. Fernando wears comfortable clothes and a pair of slippers. Sarita and Fela dress as in the scene before.

SARITA: Well, I don't want to marry him.
FELA: Why not.
SARITA: You think I want to marry an old man like him?
FELA: Don't tell Fernando he's an old man.
SARITA: I am sorry Fernando.
FERNANDO: That's all right.
FELA: He is not pretending he is a young man.
SARITA: So, why does he want to marry me?
FELA: Because I asked him. I asked him and he said yes.
SARITA: Well, nobody asked me.
FELA: Shhhh. Nobody has to ask you.
SARITA: I'm not going to be his wife.

(*Fela puts her finger to her mouth.*)

FERNANDO: I am not going to marry her if she talks like that.
FELA: Did you hear? Be nice. Sit up straight.
FERNANDO: A man my age also has a need for affection. I'm lonely. Don't think only young people need affection.
FELA: You're not so lonely, Fernando, you live here with us. And you don't stay in your room all the time. You sit here with us. You eat with us like you are a part of the family and you sit in the livingroom and you listen to the radio. And you talk to us all the time. So don't tell me you are lonely because you are not.
FERNANDO:
I'm lonely. (*He sings "I'm Lonely."*)

I am saying that I'm lonely.
I'm saying that I am alone.
Don't tell me that I am not.
I'm lonely and I know
I'm lonely and I am alone.

FELA: So, what are you trying to say?

FERNANDO: I'm trying to say that I am lonely. And I want somebody in my room.

FELA & SARITA:
He's lonely.
He is saying that he's lonely.
He's saying that he is alone.
Don't tell him that he's not.
He's lonely and he knows.
He's lonely and he is alone.

FERNANDO: If I'm going to marry her she has to be polite and she has to move into my room.

FELA: What for?

FERNANDO: To keep me company.

FELA: She can keep you company in the livingroom, not in your bedroom.

FERNANDO: Well, then I will not marry her.

SARITA: I am not keeping him company. He is boring.

FERNANDO: You see what I mean? She's rude and she's a brat. I don't want to marry her.

FELA: She doesn't want to marry you either, I just want you to marry her so her kid is legal, so she's not an unwed mother.

FERNANDO: Let her be an unwed mother.

SARITA: That's what I said.

FELA: You should be ashamed.

SARITA: Well, I'm not ashamed.

FELA: We have to make an arrangement.

FERNANDO: What kind of arrangement?

SARITA: I'm not making any arrangement.

FERNANDO: Neither am I.

SARITA: That's right.

FELA: You have to make an arrangement, you can't have everything your way. (*To Fernando.*) What arrangement.

FERNANDO: Well, in winter when it's cold, one would like a warm body to feel warm.

SARITA: I am not going to keep your body warm. I have other plans.

FELA: What plans?

SARITA: I'm going to law school.

FELA: What?

SARITA: Why not?

FELA: Law school!

SARITA: I am going to move downtown.

FELA: You can't move downtown.

SARITA: Why not?

FELA: Because I said you can't.

SARITA: I'm moving in with Yeye then.

FELA: What's the point of that?

SARITA: I don't want to get married. I am going to school.

FERNANDO: You can't go to school anymore.

SARITA: Why not?

FERNANDO: Because you are pregnant and you should be ashamed of yourself.

SARITA: I am going to law school to be a lawyer.

FERNANDO: That's for men.

SARITA: So what?—I'll study medicine.

FERNANDO: You can't.

SARITA: Why?

FERNANDO: You have to start when you're little.

SARITA: You don't study medicine when you're little.

FERNANDO: You do. You start when you're little.

SARITA: You don't know anything about medicine, Fernando.—All right, I'll study something else.

FERNANDO: What?

SARITA: I don't know. I'll join the army.

FERNANDO: You can't.

SARITA: Why not?

FERNANDO: They don't want children there.

SARITA: I'll join the navy.

FELA: Stop talking nonsense. You'll have to get married.

SARITA: Well, I won't.

FELA: I already got a license.

SARITA: Well, you can return it.

FELA: And you are not ashamed?

SARITA: No.

FELA: (*To Fernando.*) Can we return it?

FERNANDO: I don't know. (*To Sarita.*) And how are you going to study? That takes money.

SARITA: It does? I won't study then.

FERNANDO: You'll get married then?

SARITA: Not to you.

FERNANDO: I don't want to marry you either.

SARITA: Why not?

FERNANDO: Because you're a brat.

SARITA: So are you. You're a brat.

FERNANDO: I'm too old to be a brat.

SARITA: You're an old brat. A cranky old brat.

FERNANDO: That's because I need companionship.
I need some sweetness in my life.
Don't tell me that I don't.
I need to have
somebody of my own.
I need someone who'll tuck me in.
Someone who'll guard my sleep.
Someone who'll ask me how I feel.

FELA: I ask you how you feel and Sara asks you how you feel. Don't tell us we don't ask you how you feel.

FERNANDO: You don't ask me enough.

FELA: We'll ask you more often.

SARITA & FELA:
He's lonely.
He is saying that he's lonely.
He's saying that he is alone.
Don't tell him that he's not.
He's lonely and he knows.
He's lonely and he is alone.

SARITA: I know what I'm going to do. I'll go to work and support my kid. I'll go to work and that's that. I said what I have to say.

FERNANDO: Listen to her talk.

FELA: Who is going to take care of your baby?

SARITA: You. That's why you're my mother. (*To Fernando.*) And you too. That's why you live here.

FERNANDO: Is that so?

SARITA: That's right. I'll support him. So that's that. You heard what I said. (*To Fela.*) You take care of him. (*To Fernando.*) *And you too. And I'll support him.*

(*Lights fade to black. Music is heard.*)

Scene 4
1940—Fela's Song

Fela's livingroom. Fela is sitting on the couch. She dresses as in the scene before.

FELA: (*She sings "A Woman Like Me."*)
You spend your life

waiting for the first love.
You hope that first love
will come back.
But he's gone
away.

A woman like me
falls in love
with a man,
and she hopes
some day he'll come back.

She hopes
that one day
a letter
will come
with the words
"I'll return."

But that young man
ran away from her.
He travelled the world
as a merchant marine.
He drank till he fell
as he tried to forget
all he left behind.

She remembers the day
that he said,
"I love you."
The day that he said "Be my own."
The day that he kissed her till dawn.
The day that she gave him her soul.

A woman like me,
loves a man,
only one,
and he must
run away.
He must forsake her.
He must forget her.
He must betray her.
And he must drink
And die alone.

(Lights fade to black. Music is heard.)

Scene 5
1942—Sarita Leaves

Sarita is 16 years old. She has a bundle of clothes under her arm. She leans over Fela who has fallen asleep on the chair to the left. On the couch there is a teddy bear. The lights are very dim. Fela dresses as in the scene before. Sarita wears a coat and beret. Sarita speaks to Fela in a low voice. Fela does not awaken.

SARITA: . . . Mami . . . I'm leaving. Julio is back and I'm going with him. I have to, Mami. He wants me to go with him. Mami don't be angry. Take care of Melo. I'll write to you. I'll send him money. Don't worry, Mami. I'll take care of myself.

(She starts to exit. Lights fade to black. Music is heard.)

Scene 6
1942—The Mirror

The next day. Sarita and Julio are seen in the upper level. They sit side by side with their arms around each other. They face front and smile tenderly as if they are looking at each other in a mirror. Sarita wears a dress and beret. Julio wears a double breasted suit. There is drum music playing. Lights fade to black.

Scene 7
1943—1st Letter

Sarita's kitchen in a tenement building. Sarita is 17 years old. She sits at the table and reads out loud from a letter she has just written. There is another chair facing the right side of the table. Sarita and Julio wear the same clothes as in the scene before.

SARITA: Julio, you left and here I am. You are a son of a bitch and did not appreciate my love. You did this too many times already and this is the last time. I don't care, I'm doing fine. It's you who will suffer. *(She writes as she speaks the following.)* I'm going to put a curse on you. *(She reads.)* You cannot treat me like this.—Sarita. *(She props the letter on the table. She looks at it and kisses it. She props the letter up. She turns it so it will face the door. She waits. A few seconds later footsteps are heard. She quickly exits left. There is a knock on the door. There is silence. There is another knock.*) Come in!

JULIO: (*Kicking.*) Open up!

SARITA: Come in!

JULIO: The door is locked! Open it! I don't have the key.

SARITA: (*Enters, tiptoes across, opens the door and returns to the left still on tiptoe.*) How come you don't have your key?

JULIO: (*Enters.*) I don't know how come I don't have my key. (*He goes over to Sarita and tries to kiss her. She scurries to the right corner. He turns the chair to face her and sits. He opens his fly and lowers his suspenders as he speaks.*) Come here, sit on my lap.

SARITA: No.

JULIO: Come here. I'm hot.

SARITA: No.

JULIO: Hey! How come you say no?

SARITA: Look behind you.

JULIO: (*Sees the note and takes it.*) What does it say?

SARITA: Read it.

JULIO: I can't read that. It's not clear. You don't write clear. Read it to me, but read it quick because I want to kiss you.

SARITA: You just read it.

JULIO: O.K. (*He starts to read. He sneaks looks in her direction.*) Hey, honey, you look cute.

SARITA: Did you read it?

JULIO: Hey, honey, look at me.

SARITA: What for?

JULIO: Give me a kiss.

SARITA: Never mind.

JULIO: Come here. Sit on my lap.

SARITA: What for?

JULIO: For nothing.

(*Sarita straddles him. They kiss. Her pelvis moves.*)

SARITA: Why are you the way you are? Why are you so sweet and so juicy and so bad?

(*The lights fade to black. Sarita emits orgasmic sounds. There are the sounds of struggle and a fall. Julio speaks in the dark.*)

JULIO: Come here! Come here, cono.

(*The stage is lit. Sarita stands on the up left corner. Julio kneels on the floor. He holds on to her.*)

JULIO: Come here. I didn't come yet.
SARITA: Tough luck! You're a son of a bitch and I'm leaving you.
JULIO: Look at me. I want you.
SARITA: No.
JULIO: O.K., come and kiss me good bye.
SARITA: Not me. I'm not kissing you. (*She gives him a kiss. Then another and another. He lets himself be kissed.*) Oh, honey, why are you so good to kiss?
JULIO: I don't know.

(*The lights fade to black. The stage is lit again. Julio stands against the wall up right. His pants hang around his hips. Sarita sits on the chair to the right.*)

JULIO: O.K., so kiss me good bye.

(*She goes to him, puts her hand on his pelvis and kisses his neck. The lights fade to black. Music is heard.*)

Scene 8
1943—2nd Letter

Six months later. Sarita is 17 years old. She sits at the kitchen table. She writes. She reads what she has written. Sarita and Julio wear the same clothes as in the scene before.

SARITA: Julio, you left and you don't care how lonely I feel. You don't know what it is to have this happen to you and that's why you do it. Being here alone is like being in a grave. You are a son of a bitch and you don't care if I die. I feel sorry for you because you have no heart. Maybe I am a jerk and you are right. Maybe I should have never loved you or anyone. Maybe I should just do whatever comes my way and that's better, because what's the use, life stinks anyway. Good bye, Julio, let me tell you that you died in my heart and I feel sorry for you.— If you come here and you see this note just leave the keys on the table because I don't want you here again.

(*There is the sound of a key in the lock. The door opens. It is Julio. He walks to her. She puts her arms around his waist. He notices the letter, picks it up, crumples it and kisses her. The lights fade to black. Music is heard.*)

Scene 9
1944—3rd Letter

Six months later. Sarita is 18 years old. She sits at the kitchen table. She writes. She reads what she has written. She wears the same clothes as in the scene before.

SARITA: Julio, when you come in and you see this note you are going to laugh as you always do because you'll think I'm going to forgive you and maybe you're right that I have no will power when it comes to you, and that I am an old rag and that that's why you have no respect for me. I have no respect for me either.—I know I cannot trust myself. When I am with you I don't care about anything and I hate myself for that. I can't live any longer because I hate myself. I'm going to die Julio and I don't care what you think. I'm doing it because I hate myself and what I am. It is awful not to have pride—I'm not doing it because I love you because this is not love.—It's like a sickness that lives in my heart and I have tried to tear it out but I can't. I am sick with it and I want to die. May God help me. I hope my baby can forgive me. And I hope my Mami understands. Good bye.

(She puts the note down, puts on her coat and exits. Lights fade to black. Music is heard.)

Scene 10
1944—Empire State Building

A few hours later. There is a backdrop which depicts the Empire State Building. Sarita stands to the left. Mark stands to the right. They both face front and look down. Sarita wears a coat. Mark wears a soldier's uniform.

SARITA: Hey. You. *(Mark looks up.)* Move aside.
MARK: What?
SARITA: Move. *(Short pause.)* Get out of the way.
MARK: What for?
SARITA: I'm going to jump. *(He looks at her.)* Are you going to move?

(There is a pause.)

MARK: No.
SARITA: Move or I'll fall on you.
MARK: Why do you want to jump?

SARITA: Move or I'm going to fall on you. (*Mark takes a step to the side.*) Move further. (*He takes another step. She signals with her hand.*) More. (*He takes another step.*) More. (*She gestures.*) More.

MARK: I'm up against the wall.

SARITA: Move to this side then.

(*Mark does. There is a pause.*)

MARK: Why do you want to jump? (*Sarita begins to whimper.*) Can I come up? (*She doesn't answer.*) Will you wait till I get up? (*She nods. He turns to face her.*) What's wrong? (*She lowers her head and remains silent.*) May I come closer? (*She nods. He moves closer.*) Don't cry. (*She looks at him.*) You want to come have some coffee with me? (*She nods. He takes her by the arm. They take a step together. She changes her mind, moves away, then walks to him.*)

SARITA: I want to die.

MARK: Why?

SARITA: Because I am miserable.

MARK: Why?

SARITA: Because I am jealous. Jealous! Jealous! Jealousy that tears me apart and I want to die. He has no respect for me. He takes advantage of me. He mistreats me.

MARK: Does he hit you?

SARITA: Who?

MARK: He.

SARITA: Let him dare. If he hits me I'll kill him.—He is untrue. He betrays me. Anyone can take him from me. Anyone. And I die. Each time he does it I die.—He is not mine. I keep him. But he is not mine. He dishonors me.—Don't you see? I keep him. I work hard. He doesn't work. He's always planning to start work. But there's always something.—He steps all over me. I am dishonored. I don't want to live. (*She looks at him.*) You are so nice.—You are so nice.—I know you're nice.

(*He has fallen in love.*)

MARK: (*He sings "You Are Tahiti."*)
You are the flower.
I am the snow.
You are Tahiti.
I am Gauguin.

You are all color
I am the brush.

I, without you,
am but a void.

You are the flower.
I am the snow.
You are Tahiti.
I am Gauguin.

I am the vessel
that fills with nectar
at your approach.

You are my joy
You are my joy
My love
My joy.

SARITA: Do you know that . . . that without you I would have died?

(The lights fade to black. There is music.)

ACT TWO

Scene 11
1944—The Party

Two months later. Fela's livingroom. Sarita is 18 years old. She and Fela decorate an altar to Oshun (the Virgin of La Caridad del Cobre). They wear party clothes. There are conga drums on the up left corner of the stage.

SARITA: I met an American boy and I like him. He is shy and very sweet. He thinks I am the greatest thing in the world and he takes me out. We go where I want. He is always smiling. He likes me, you know. I know he likes me. He brings me flowers, like the old sweethearts. He brings them to be funny, but he still brings them. He's very cute. He has a pink nose. He's a cutie pie. He's a baby. He's young for me. I'm not older, but I have been through things. We go dancing. And he's not bad. He has his rhythm and his little smile.

(Pointing to her side. She sings "A Little Boo Boo.")

And here.
I have a boo-boo.

(Pointing each time to different parts of her body.)

Put a little kiss here
another here.
Take away this boo-boo
this boo-boo du du du

boo du du du
boo du
here

Put a little kiss . . .
another here.
Take away this boo-boo
today.
Put your lips there,
Papi.

(*Sarita puts her hand on her breast.*)
FELA: Niña!
SARITA & FELA:
Ay Mami, but it feels good
when he kisses me.
Put a little kiss here
Good bye little boo-boo.
boo du du du
du du du du
boo du du du
du du du du.
Another boo-boo
Good bye, pain.

(*They dance a jitterbug. At the end of the song Sarita sits left and Fela returns to the fixing of the altar. Yeye enters carrying two bowls. She wears a party dress.*)

YEYE: Which one do you want?
FELA: Both.

(*Yeye sits to the right. Fernando enters carrying a plate with fritters in a paper bag and flowers. He wears a suit and tie.*)

FERNANDO: (*Giving the flowers to Fela.*) Here are the flowers and here are the fritters. But I want to make it clear that I don't believe in all this espiritismo and santeria. I'm a Catholic and I don't see why you have to give food to the Virgin.
FELA: That's Oshun, Fernando.
FERNANDO: That's a statue of the Virgin Mary.
FELA: Yes, but it's Oshun. Give me the fritters.

(*There is a knock on the door. Sarita goes to open it.*)

FERNANDO: And why do you have to feed her? Do you think she's going to come down and eat the food? She has no teeth.

FELA: When you put flowers in church, do you think the saints come down to smell them?

FERNANDO: No, but they like that you do.

FELA: Well, Oshun likes that I feed her. Kneel down and pray, Fernando. You're splitting hairs. (*He does. Juan and Sarita enter. Sarita stands behind Yeye's chair and leans on it.*) Hello Juan. You came just in time.

JUAN: Hello Fela. La bendición.

FELA: Que Dios te bendiga. We were just going to teach Fernando how to pray.

JUAN: Maybe if I say a prayer to Oshun it would inspire Don Fernando.

FELA: That would be good.

JUAN: (*Kneels in front of the altar. He sings "Ofe Isia."*)
Oshun yeye.
Oshun yeye.
Librame de Ado
Librame de Ofu
También de Araye
Para que todo sea oye
Para que todo sea yeye.

(*He puts his hand on Fernando's head.*)

Ebofi Eboada

(*He stands, goes to the drums and plays.*)

Ofe isia. Ofe isia.

FERNANDO: Ofe isia. Ofe isia.

JUAN: Oshun y cole. Ofe isia

CHORUS: Ofe isia

JUAN: Elade Oshun osha mina la yeo

CHORUS: Elade Oshun

(*The women start dancing.*)

JUAN: Osha mina la yeo

CHORUS: Elade Oshun

JUAN: Eko lare lare

CHORUS: Eko eko

JUAN: Lare lare

CHORUS: Eko eko

JUAN: Oma oma oke oke

CHORUS: Oma oma oke oke
JUAN: Yeye moro
CHORUS: Oma oma oke oke

(*Fela and Sarita dance. Fernando sits on the chair on the left. Toward the end of the dance Mark enters and joins Sarita in the dance. The drum music ends. A foxtrot starts. Mark and Sarita dance. Fela sits on the couch.*)

MARK: Hm. . . .
SARITA: Hm. . . .
MARK: You're a tropical beauty.
SARITA: And you . . .
MARK: Me?
SARITA: You are a beauty from I don't know where.
MARK: I'm not a beauty.
SARITA: Where are you from?
MARK: From Cleveland.
SARITA: And in Cleveland all the fellows look like you?
MARK: No.
SARITA: I knew they didn't. They couldn't. You're too cute. What do they look like?
MARK: They all look different.
SARITA: Do they all smile like you?
MARK: No.
SARITA: What do they smile like? (*He makes a face. There is a knock on the door. Yeye goes to open it.*) And what do they say when they like a girl?
MARK: They say Oo! Loo-loo-loo-loo-loo!
SARITA: And is it true that they are all preachers' sons?
MARK: Yes.
SARITA: And is it true that they are all evangelists?
MARK: Yes.

(*Julio and Yeye enter. Yeye returns to her chair. Julio carries a box of chocolates which he gives to Fela. He turns to watch the couple dance. He nods to Fernando.*)

SARITA: And what do they dance?
MARK: They jitterbug.
SARITA: Oh, yes?
MARK: Uh huh.
SARITA: And what else?

MARK: (*Producing a corsage of flowers.*) We bring flowers to the ladies.
SARITA: Are those boys marvelous?
MARK: Yes.
SARITA: Hm. That's nice.

(*They dance a moment longer. The music ends. Sarita walks toward the altar. She sees Julio and drops the flowers.*)

JULIO: Go ahead, dance, dance. I don't care if you dance.
SARITA: I don't care if you dance either. Go ahead dance.—I was dancing before you came. I didn't ask you if I could. Did I?
JULIO: That's true. But I think you should.
SARITA: Sure, but you weren't here. That's why I went ahead and did it. I would have waited for you to appear, but I didn't know if you were alive.
JULIO: Well, I said it's all right if you dance. Why do you have to get like that?
SARITA: Because you don't have to give me permission to dance. (*Doing a dance step.*) Look! I don't need your permission.
JULIO: I just thought you may want to know that I think it's all right.
SARITA: Sure. Let me know any time you think it's all right. I'm very interested.

(*She exits. Mark approaches Julio.*)

JULIO: How do you do. I am very glad to meet you. I heard a lot about you. I was looking forward to meeting you. You look like you are in business. What kind of business are you in?
MARK: What kind of business are you in?
JULIO: What do you mean?
MARK: What line of business?
JULIO: I'm on relief.
MARK: Are you disabled?
JULIO: Yes. Not able to work.
MARK: Why not?
JULIO: I need free time.
MARK: For what?
JULIO: To do nothing.
MARK: Don't you think you should be in the service?
JULIO: Oh no. I'm too busy.
MARK: Doing what?
JULIO: I do some things.
MARK: What?

JULIO: I'm a pickpocket. (*He puts his hands in Mark's trouser pockets and starts emptying his pockets.*) See?

MARK: Wait a moment.

JULIO: It's all right. It's all right. (*He starts emptying Mark's jacket pockets.*)

FELA: Julio!

SARITA: (*Entering.*) What's the matter?

JULIO: See? This is how I do it.—I don't want to hurt you. I just want to get all your money.

MARK: (*Grabbing Julio by the arm.*) Cut that out.

FELA: Stop that.

MARK: Come outside. I don't want to hit you here. Come outside.

FELA: Stop that! Both of you! (*Sarita pushes Mark to the right. Yeye and Fernando push Julio to the left.*) Cut that out Julio. You'll have to leave if you act like that.

JULIO: Business! Business! You're nothing but a clean shirt! A clean shirt! (*Fela takes Mark out. Juan, Yeye and Fernando exit.*) What is he! A clean shirt. Nothing but a clean shirt! A clean shirt! A clean shirt!

(*Sarita picks up Mark's belongings from the floor and is about to exit. Julio speaks to her. She turns and looks at Julio. They stare at each other through the following. Mark's shadow appears in the up left window.*)

MARK: (*He sings "His Wonderful Eye."*)
For the lord
speaks in the darkness,
shines in the shadow,
walks in the swamp.

For the lord
came to the valley,
walked in the forest,
brightened the sky.

And I see his eye,
and his eye says come to me.
And I see his face,
and his face says follow me.

(*Sarita exits. Julio walks to the right and faces front.*)

And I see his wonderful eye
looking, looking at me.

—See his wonderful eye
looking, looking at me.

(*The light in the window fades.*)

JULIO: (*Speaking front.*) I don't work! O.K.! I don't like to work!—You
don't work on Sunday and you think that's smart. Well, it's not. I don't
work all week. That's smarter! For me every day is Sunday. Monday's
Sunday. Tuesday's Sunday. Wednesday's Sunday. That's smarter. You
go to the factory.—I hang around the street. So, maybe I die
young—so maybe. I'm not spending my life in a factory. (*Sarita appears on the up left door. Julio turns to her and points.*) Not for you,
and not for anyone.

(*Music starts. They walk to center. They dance and sing. There is a spot
on them.*)

JULIO: (*He sings "Here Comes the Night."*)
Here comes the chill,
I feel it moving
deep into my bones
and as I hold you in my arms
I know that I have lost you,
Now I know that I am done.
SARITA:
Here comes the still,
the deadly night
that brings the darkened time.
And as I look into your eyes
I know my heart is silent
I have laid down to die.
SARITA & JULIO:
Frozen fingers
hold the shadow
Bloodless lips
want to smile.
Icy eyes look at
the shadow
of a love that's but a ghost.

(*The lights fade to black.*)

Scene 12
1945—The Letter

Fela's livingroom. Yeye sits at the table holding a hand of cards. Fela stands in the doorway to the right. The deck of cards and Fela's hand are on the table. They wear Sunday clothes.

FELA: Teyo said, "Come when you can. I'll give you a room and food and clothes." (*She exits and returns to the doorway.*) I wrote to him that I was coming and that I was pregnant with his baby. (*She exits and returns.*) And when I arrived he wasn't here. He ran away because he didn't want to take care of me and the baby. (*She exits, returns with a cup of coffee and sits.*) I had no money and no place to sleep. Are you sure you don't want coffee?

YEYE: I'm sure.

FELA: And I almost had no clothes because I came with what I had which was almost nothing. When I arrived they told me he no longer lived there, that he had gotten work on a boat and that he said he was not coming back.

YEYE: And what did you do?

FELA: Nothing. I couldn't do anything. (*There is a pause.*) I stayed there in the hallway. I stood against the wall and didn't move for a long time. I didn't know where to go. Later the super came and he asked me if I had no place to go and his wife brought me a plate of food. And then she asked me to go in the apartment and she asked me if I had no one to call. I didn't and they said I could sleep there if I wanted to.

YEYE: Did he ever come back?

FELA: (*She shakes her head.*) Sometime after I heard he was back home. He was sick. And he died. I didn't mourn him. It felt different not thinking he was alive someplace. Something went empty inside me. But I didn't cry for him. I didn't tell Sarita her dad was dead. I'll tell her sometime. So she knows that her dad is buried someplace. It may be that she needs to know that.

YEYE: That her dad is dead?

FELA: Yes, maybe she needs to know that.

YEYE: You never saw him, then?

FELA: No. Never. You don't want coffee?

YEYE: O.K.

(*Fela exits and returns with a cup of coffee. She sits.*)

YEYE: You know who I saw the other day?

FELA: Who?

YEYE: Sister Clara.

FELA: How is she?

YEYE: She looked good.

FELA: She was strict.

YEYE: She wasn't as bad as she appeared to be. She talked to us about things. She talked about obedience. She said that obedience was beneficial to the spirit. That it was conducive to spiritual growth.

FELA: I know. Tell that to Sarita.

YEYE: She knows it. She used to listen to Sister Clara like I did. She'd go on her knees and cry and say, I want to be obedient, Yeye. I want to obey. I want to be obedient. I want to obey I want to obey I want to obey I want to obey I want to obey.

FELA: Yes, I know. (*They play their cards.*) . . . Why did Mario say what he said?

YEYE: About what?

FELA: About the baby.

YEYE: He said he didn't want a girl.

FELA: Did he say that?

YEYE: Yes.

FELA: And what is he going to do if you have a girl?

YEYE: Nothing. He said he'll leave.

FELA: And what are you going to do if he leaves?

YEYE: I don't know Fe. He's going to leave anyway. I know he's going to leave whether he leaves me now or he leaves me later. Whether he leaves me because I have a girl or just because he wants to leave. He's going to go anyway.—I want to have a baby just the same. (*She smiles.*) I want to have a baby. Men are like that, Fe. They don't want a family. They don't feel like women that they want to have a baby. I want to have a baby. Have a little baby in my arms. Men don't have that need and they get frightened when their women start having babies. For them it's a weight on their backs. It's being chained. For women too it's being chained. But they don't mind. They want the baby and it's part of them. Things are tough for women.—They are tough for men too because they don't understand it.—To them it's just a weight on their backs. It's not their fault, that's how God made them. Is it their fault? If they are that way it must be for a reason. (*Taking an envelope from her pocket.*) I got this in the mail. (*She puts it on the table.*)

FELA: What is it?

YEYE: It's from Julio. Inside there's an envelope that says "for Sara."

FELA: Why are you telling me?

YEYE: Because I don't know what to do with it. I don't know if I should give it to her.

FELA: Well . . . I don't know either.—Don't give it to her. Throw it out.

YEYE: . . . I don't know what to do with it.

FELA: Well, don't leave it there.

YEYE: (*She puts the letter in the couch, between a cushion and the arm. Going back to her chair.*) If she sees it she sees it. If she doesn't she doesn't.

FELA: Play, it's your turn.

(*They start to play.*)

YEYE: At what time are they coming?

FELA: They should be here soon.

YEYE: Are they going to get married?

FELA: (*Shrugs her shoulders.*) He wanted to and she didn't want to. Then she wanted and he didn't want to.

YEYE: Why not?

FELA: Time passes and men lose their interest.

YEYE: He's lost interest?

FELA: No, he's interested. I don't know why he didn't want to get married. I don't understand them. They're not like they used to be. They're complicated. Their reasons are always different than what they used to be. You think I understand them. Do you understand them? The war changed things. I don't understand young people anymore. Play.

YEYE: Are Melo and Mark still good friends?

FELA: Oh, yes.

YEYE: Is he with them now?

FELA: No, he's out with Fernando. They went to buy shoes.

YEYE: For Melo?

FELA: For Fernando. He wanted Melo's opinion.

YEYE: Fernando is nice to him.

FELA: He thinks he is his father.

YEYE: You should marry him.

FELA: Are you crazy?

YEYE: Everybody thinks you live together anyway.

FELA: They do?

YEYE: Sure.

FELA: Who does?

YEYE: Everybody. Anybody in the block.

FELA: Hm. (*The doorbell rings.*) Here they are.

(*Sarita and Mark enter. Sarita is 19 years old. She carries a large box. Mark carries a bag of groceries. They wear Sunday clothes. They kiss at the door.*)

SARITA: Hello, hello. (*Kiss.*)

FELA: Hello. (*Kiss.*)

SARITA: Where's Melo.

FELA: He's with Fernando. Hello, Mark. (*Kiss.*)

SARITA: I got him the truck. Where did they go?

MARK: Hello. (*Kiss.*)

FELA: Give me your coats.—To get shoes for Fernando. He wanted Melo's opinion.

MARK: Sure. Melo has good taste.

SARITA: (*Walking to Yeye.*) Yeye, how are you? (*They kiss.*)

YEYE: Fine . . . fine. How are you? How are you, Mark?

SARITA: Fine.

MARK: I'm fine.

FELA: You look good. You're putting on some weight.

MARK: Yeah, I have to go on a diet.

FELA: Don't go on a diet. You don't need to go on a diet. You're still too skinny. Guess what I'm making?

MARK: What?

FELA: Black beans.

MARK: I had my heart set on that.

SARITA: She knows how to get to him.

FELA: And platanos.

MARK: How soon?

FELA: Soon. And lechón.

MARK: I can't bear it.

FELA: We'll finish the game and then we'll eat.

SARITA: What are you playing?

YEYE: Brisca.

SARITA: Well, I don't play that.

YEYE: We could play something else.

SARITA: (*Putting her hand on Yeye's stomach.*) How does it feel?

YEYE: Wonderful.

SARITA: I'm so glad.

YEYE: I'm too.

FELA: You want something to drink?

SARITA: (*To Fela.*) We brought beer. And bread and coquitos.—When are they coming?

FELA: Melo?

SARITA: Yes.

FELA: Soon. They'll be here soon.—I have pasteles too.

SARITA: That's good. (*She lies on the couch.*) We'll have plenty to eat.

FELA: Come, Mark, taste this.

(*Mark exits. Sarita feels the letter with her hand and pulls it out.*)

SARITA: (*Putting the letter on the table.*) This was on the side of the couch. (*She leans over to glance at the envelope.*) That looks like . . . (*She stops short and looks at Yeye questioningly.*) It's addressed to you.
YEYE: It's for you.

(*Sarita opens the letter. Mark enters.*)

MARK: What is it?
SARITA: A letter for Yeye I found on the couch.

(*Yeye puts the letter in her pocket. Mark sits.*)

MARK: Shall we play?
YEYE: (*Picking up the cards.*) What do you want to play?
MARK: Let's play rummy.

(*Yeye shuffles the cards and deals.*)

FELA: Do you want some beer, Mark?
MARK: Yes, thank you.
FELA: You, Sara?
SARITA: I'll get it. (*She exits.*)

(*Mark, Yeye, and Sarita sing "The Letter."*)

MARK:
  What is that you've got in your pocket?
YEYE:
  It's nothing.
MARK:
  Let me see what you've got in your pocket.
YEYE:
  It's nothing. It's personal.
MARK:
  A letter from your boyfriend?
YEYE:
  Mark, I don't have a boyfriend.
MARK:
  Oh, no?
  (*Mark takes the letter and crushes it in his hand.*)
YEYE:
  Mark, let me have that letter.
MARK:
  Sara does.

YEYE:

Don't do that. Don't do that please!

MARK:

I'm not kidding. She has a boyfriend.
Her true love.

YEYE:

Don't say that.

MARK:

You don't know that?

YEYE:

Please, Mark.

MARK:

Don't worry. You could pass letters
between them any time you want to.

YEYE:

Please stop.

MARK:

They'll trust you. It isn't like you told me
"This is what's happening, Mark. I got this
in the mail."

YEYE:

Let me have the letter.

MARK:

You didn't say that.
(Tearing the first envelope off.)
You didn't say that.
So you have nothing to worry about.
(Tearing the second envelope open and taking out the letter.)
Let's see what it says.
(Putting the letter to his nose.)
Is it perfumed? Oh, what a pity. It isn't.
It's not that kind of romance.
(He opens it.)
Let's see.

SARITA: *(Entering.)*

What have I done?

MARK:

Let's see.
(Throwing the letter at her.)
Here! It's a letter from your lover!
(He grabs his coat.)

SARITA:

What have I done to make you speak this way
to me?

MARK:
  Your lover! See what he wants!
SARITA:
  What are you thinking of?
MARK:
  What does he want! What does the darling want?
SARITA:
  What are you thinking of
  (*Mark exits. His voice is heard in the distance.*)
MARK:
  What does he want! What does your lover want!
  What does he want! What does he want!
  What does he want! Read his letter!
  Read his letter! What does he want?
SARITA:
  What have I done?
  What are you thinking of?
  I have not seen him since I've been with you.

(*Lights fade to black. Music is heard.*)

Scene 13
1945—Summer Resort

Six months later. A summer resort. Sarita sits on a beach chair. She is sunning herself. There is an empty chair next to her. Mark enters and sits. Through the following speech he takes off his shoes, socks, and shirt. He rolls up his pants and lies back. Sarita wears the skirt of her previous dress and a halter. Mark wears pants and a Hawaiian shirt.

SARITA: What happened?
MARK: Someone passed out.
SARITA: Who?
MARK: A woman.
SARITA: What happened to her?
MARK: I don't know. I couldn't get near her. There was a crowd around her.
SARITA: She probably ate and went in the water.
MARK: (*Surprised.*) That's what they were saying.
SARITA: Maybe that's what happened.
MARK: Why would someone pass out from that?
SARITA: From eating and going in the water?
MARK: Yes.

SARITA: You didn't know one could die from that?

MARK: Why would anyone die from that?

SARITA: You must be kidding.

MARK: I'm not kidding. Can you die from that?

SARITA: Sure. You get a congestion and die.

MARK: What is that?

SARITA: A congestion? You don't know what that is?

MARK: No.

SARITA: That's what you get when you go in the water after you eat.

MARK: Come on.

SARITA: You can also die if you drink cold beer or a cold drink after you eat too much on a hot day.

MARK: And what do you call that?

SARITA: Empacho.

MARK: That sounds like a tango. Tango empache.

SARITA: That's apache. Tango apache. I hope you don't catch an empacho and die.

MARK: We don't have empacho in this country.

SARITA: You do. You just don't know what it's called.

MARK: We don't. In English we don't die if we drink cold beer after a meal.

SARITA: You could also die if you take a shower after a meal . . . or a bath. You can kick a leg and that sounds like a conga. You kick your leg when you do a conga. You think empacho sounds like a tango, but kick a leg sounds like a conga.

MARK: You can die from doing a conga?

SARITA: No, you can't die from doing a conga but neither does empacho sound like a tango.

MARK: Well, I don't think she went in the water. She was fully dressed.

SARITA: Maybe she put her feet in the water.

MARK: Maybe. She was wearing shoes though.

SARITA: Well, maybe she fell in.

MARK: Well, maybe.

SARITA: Was she wet?

MARK: I don't know. I didn't see any water.

SARITA: Maybe the water had dried.

MARK: Maybe.

SARITA: Well, if she didn't fall in the water, what did she die of?

MARK: I don't think she died.

SARITA: Well, you don't know how to do a conga, anyway.

MARK: Yes, I do. Anyone can do a conga. (*He moves his feet as if doing a conga.*)

SARITA: Maybe. (*Short pause.*)

MARK: You don't take a shower after a meal?
SARITA: No.
MARK: I do.
SARITA: It's a wonder you're alive.

(*Lights fade to black. Music is heard.*)

Scene 14
1945—Prayer

A few days later. In Fela's livingroom. Sarita kneels facing front. She looks up. She wears the same dress as in Scene 12.

SARITA: If one has one love in one's lifetime, only one, and one has been true to that love, does one go straight to heaven?—for being true? (*Short pause.*) I hope so. Because here it's hell. (*Short pause.*) I just want to know if you know about this? (*Short pause.*) Is this your idea?—Or is the devil doing it? (*Short pause.*) Give me a sign. (*Short pause.*) Say something. (*Short pause.*) Go on. (*Short pause.*) Do something. (*She palms her hand as if there were a small person in it. She lowers her voice.*) Good Lord, child, somebody made a mistake. I put you in for an easy life. You're my favorite kid. Don't worry about a thing, honey. I'll take care of things. (*Using her own voice.*) Oh, God! Thank you God.—God. I am serious. I cannot breathe. I'm burning. I'm turned inside myself. Do you know what I'm saying?—I feel my life's leaving me. I feel I'm dying. God, I want to love Mark and no one else.

(*Lights fade to black. Music is heard.*)

Scene 15
1946—I Don't Love You

Sarita's kitchen. Sarita is 20 years old. She sits to the right of the kitchen table. Julio sits on the floor against the right wall. Their clothes are dishevelled.

SARITA: No. I don't love you. I don't love you.
JULIO: You don't. Didn't you love me a moment ago? Didn't you?
SARITA: No.
JULIO: Oh no. You didn't.

SARITA: No.

JULIO: Oh no?

SARITA: No.

JULIO: And what was that that happened just now. What was that?

SARITA: I don't know. I lost my mind. (*He goes to her and takes her arm.*) Let go.

JULIO: Baby.

SARITA: Let me be. (*He takes a step away and stops. There is a pause.*) What was it you wanted?

JULIO: A kiss.

SARITA: O.K.—Come here if you want it. (*He goes to her.*) Take it.

(*He kisses her. Lights fade to black. Music is heard.*)

Scene 16
1946—By the Window

A few days later. Fernando sits in Fela's livingroom. The lights are dim. The light of dusk is seen through the windows. Sarita enters. She wears the same dress as in the scene before. Fernando wears pants and a sweater.

SARITA: Fernando . . . (*Pause.*) Why do you sit in the dark?—Should I turn the light on?

FERNANDO: Oh, no. It's still light outside.

SARITA: Doesn't it bother you to sit in the dark? (*Pause.*) What do you think of when you sit like this?

FERNANDO: I don't think much. I rest.

SARITA: Won't you rest better lying down?

FERNANDO: No, I like to sit like this.

SARITA: When I see you sitting in the dark I think you're sad.

FERNANDO: Oh, no, I'm not.

SARITA: Do you doze off?

FERNANDO: No.

SARITA: What do you think about? Aren't you thinking anything?

FERNANDO: I imagine things.

SARITA: What?

FERNANDO: I imagine that things are peaceful. That people go to work, and come back from work, and they eat, and go to sleep.

SARITA: Is that what you think. . . ?

FERNANDO: Yes.

SARITA: You are so dear.

FERNANDO: (*He looks out.*) For many years I didn't think of the people here. I thought of my island—which was beautiful and peaceful. I sat here, but in my mind I was sitting on the porch in my parents' house. Do you do that? Do you spend time in a place that's far away?

SARITA: Yes.

FERNANDO: In my island nothing bad ever happened. A dog died once. (*He looks out.*) Then, it happened that I didn't think of my island any more. I thought of the people here. That's how I became an American. I thought of the people here. I imagined that you came from school and you did your homework and that you didn't get into fights in the street. Or go out with boys who were mean and disrespectful. That's how I became an American.

SARITA: I wish I could think like you. I think of many things, but never quiet things. My heart is restless and I think of things that hurt me. They frighten me. I feel pain in my chest. I am in danger. Teach me how to be like you. Teach me how to look for peace. My heart won't let me.

(*Lights fade to black. Music is heard.*)

Scene 17
1947—The Key

Sarita's kitchen. Mark sits at the kitchen table. He reads from a large textbook and makes notes on a yellow pad. There is the sound of a key. Mark looks toward the door. Then returns to his work. The door opens. Julio enters. Mark looks at him in a state of shock. Mark wears a shirt and pants. Julio wears a blue suit.

JULIO: I had this key here that I had to return. I didn't knock because I thought there was no one here,—and I thought I'd just leave it on the table. I thought I'd just write a note on paper and say I had the key and I thought I'd drop it off. Because I shouldn't have a key that's not the key to my place. (*He puts the key on the floor.*) Say hello to Sara.—I haven't seen her in a while.—Bye now.

(*Julio exits. Mark stares at the open door. Lights fade to black. There is the sound of music.*)

Scene 18
1947—Drinking

A few hours later. Mark sits with his head on the table. He is unconscious. There is a bottle of liquor and a shot glass on the table. Sarita enters. She is 21 years old. She starts to go to Mark, notices the key and picks it up. She is dejected. Mark and Sarita wear the same dress as when last seen. Lights fade to black. Music is heard.

Scene 19
1947—Death Scene

Three months later. Sarita's kitchen. Sarita sits. Julio is standing. She wears a slip. He is in his underwear.

JULIO: Hey, don't give me that. I need money. I have to eat. You don't want me to tell Mark—you give me some money. I'm not doing nothing wrong. So you like to hit the hay with me—so I have to eat. There's nothing wrong with that. Come on, baby. Let's do it. If you give me a few dollars I won't tell him. I need the money. Otherwise you can't eat. Don't give me that lady stuff. I know you ain't no lady. (*He goes to kiss her. She takes a knife from the table and stabs him. He speaks as he begins to fall.*) Hey, honey, what are you doing? Hey, hey, hey, hey, baby baby. Hey, baby. (*He holds on to her. They slide down to the floor. His head is on her lap. He is unconscious. She starts to sob. The rhythm of the song is set by her sobbing.*)

SARITA: (*She sings "Papi, No."*)
No . . .
No . . .
Don't leave me, Papi,
No. . . .

Papito, no.
No, Papito, Papi.
No.

Don't leave me, Papi,
Papi, no.
Don't leave me, Papi,
Papi, no.
Ay, Papito.
Ay, Papito

Ay, Papito.
No.

I love you, Papi, Papo.
Don't die.
I love you, love you, Papo.

(*She takes money out of her bosom, both coins and bills, and puts it in his hands. She tries to open his eyes.*)

Mírame, Papi.
Look at me.
Look at me, Papi.
Look at me.

With your,
With your pretty eyes, Papi.
The way I like it.
The way I like you to look at me.

Shit, Papi, look at me.
No te mueras, caray.
Please, Papi don't die.
Please, Papi, Papi, don't die.
Ay, chico, coño,
Look at me.

Give me a kiss.

(*She kisses his lips.*)

Where is your little tongue?

(*She looks at him.*)

Shit, papi.
Papi, are you dead?

(*She sobs.*)

Ay. . . .
Ay. . . .

(*Pushing him away.*)

Get away from me.
Why are you doing this?

(*She sobs.*)

Ay, Papi.
Ay, Papi.

(*She sobs. Lights fade to black. Music is heard.*)

Scene 20
1947—Mental Hospital

Three months later. A sitting room in a mental hospital. Sarita and Fernando sit facing each other. Sarita wears a hospital robe. Fernando wears a suit.

SARITA: I feel better, Fernando, a lot better. The doctor said I am better, because now I remember what happened. It hurts a lot more to remember, but the doctor says it's better even if it hurts. (*She lowers her head.*) I am glad you came. (*Pause.*) How is Mami?
FERNANDO: She's fine.
SARITA: When is she coming?
FERNANDO: Tomorrow.
SARITA: I'll like to see her.
FERNANDO: She'll be here tomorrow.
SARITA: I miss her.
FERNANDO: She was here this morning.
SARITA: She was?
FERNANDO: You don't remember?
SARITA: (*She thinks a while. She speaks softly.*) . . . I remember. . . .
FERNANDO: She comes every morning.
SARITA: . . . She does? . . .
FERNANDO: Yes. And I come afternoons.
SARITA: Every afternoon?
FERNANDO: Yes. (*Pause.*) Melo wants to come too. He said to give you this. (*He gives her a flower.*) He said, "Give this to Mami, and tell her that I love her."
SARITA: (*She speaks as if in a trance.*) Yesterday I spoke to him. He's very far. I called him collect. He said that Mami is growing tulips.
FERNANDO: Would you like to see him?
SARITA: No. I don't want him to come here. He'll cry. Mami cries all the

time. He cries with her. She cries all the time and he also cries. He is too little to cry so much. That girl makes him cry.

FERNANDO: Who?

SARITA: Sara. Don't let her near him. She's going to hurt him. Don't let her hurt him. She has done enough harm.—It's this thing I have inside me. Something I cannot tear off. It is a bad growth that will not die.

FERNANDO: (*Takes wrapped chocolate from his pocket.*) I brought you this. (*Mark enters.*) Mark is here. He came with me.

SARITA: Mark?

MARK: (*He walks to her and kneels by her side.*) Hello Sara.

SARITA: Hello Mark. How are you? (*Mark sits on a chair.*) You came to see me? (*He nods.*) Even after what happened? (*He nods.*) I knew you were nice. I always knew it. (*Pause.*) What do you think will happen? What will they do to me?

(*Mark and Sarita's hands lock with force as music is heard. Lights fade to black.*)

END

MUSIC FOR *SARITA*

Lyrics: Maria Irene Fornes   *Music: Leon Odenz, ASCAP*

"He Was Thinking of You" (Yeye) ══════════ "I'm Pudding" (Sarita)

"Holy Spirit, Good Morning" (Sarita, Yeye)

"A Woman Like Me" (Fela)

"You Are Tahiti" (Mark)

40's Type Ballad (slow 4)

YOU ARE THE FLOW-ER. I AM THE SNOW.

YOU ARE TA-HI- TI. I AM GAU-GUIN. YOU ARE ALL COL-OR

I AM THE BRUSH AND I,___ WITH-OUT YOU, AM BUT A VOID.

YOU ARE THE FLOW-ER I AM THE SNOW YOU ARE TA- HI - TI

I AM GAU-GUIN. I AM THE VESSEL THAT FILLS WITH NECTAR AT YOUR AP-

PROACH. YOU ARE MY JOY YOU ARE MY JOY MY LOVE MY JOY.

"His Wonderful Eye" (Mark)

GOSPEL (bright 2)

FOR THE LORD SPEAKS IN THE DARK-NESS, SHINES IN THE SHADOW, WALKS IN THE

SWAMP. FOR THE LORD CAME TO THE VAL-LEY, WALKED IN THE FOR-EST, BRIGHTENED THE

SKY. AND I SEE HIS___ EYE, AND HIS EYE SAYS COME TO ME. AND I

SEE HIS___ FACE, AND HIS FACE SAYS FOL-LOW ME_____. AND I

SEE HIS WONDER-FUL EYE _____, LOOK-ING, LOOK-ING AT ME__.

SEE HIS WONDER-FUL EYE_____ LOOK-ING, LOOK-ING AT ME_____.

"Here Comes the Night" (Sarita, Julio)

"The Letter" (Mark, Yeye, Sarita)

M. LOVER SEE WHAT HE WANTS   WHAT DOES HE WANT? WHAT DOES THE DARLING WANT?

S. ME   WHAT ARE YOU THINKING OF   WHAT ARE YOU

M. WHAT DOES HE WANT? WHAT DOES YOUR LOVER WANT? WHAT DOES HE WANT?

S. THINKING OF

M. WHAT DOES HE WANT? READ HIS LETTER. READ HIS LETTER.

M. WHAT DOES HE WANT___ (SARITA) WHAT HAVE I DONE   WHAT ARE YOU THINKING OF___

I HAVE NOT SEEN HIM SINCE I'VE BEEN WITH   YOU _____

"Papi, No" (Sarita)

GET A-WAY FROM ME. WHY ARE YOU DO-ING THIS? // (TPT.)

AY PA- PI- TO   AY (SCREAM)

rit.

PAJ PLAYSCRIPTS

GENERAL EDITORS: Bonnie Marranca and Gautam Dasgupta

THEATRE OF THE RIDICULOUS/Bernard, Ludlam, Tavel

ANIMATIONS: A TRILOGY FOR MABOU MINES/Lee Breuer

THE RED ROBINS/Kenneth Koch

THE WOMEN'S PROJECT 1/Gilliatt, Mueller, Goldemberg, et al.

THE WOMEN'S PROJECT 2/Cizmar, Mack, Galloway, et al.

WORDPLAYS 1: NEW AMERICAN DRAMA/Fornes, Van Itallie, et al.

WORDPLAYS 2: NEW AMERICAN DRAMA/Owens, Shawn, et al.

WORDPLAYS 3: NEW AMERICAN DRAMA/Mednick, Kennedy, Breuer, et al.

WORDPLAYS 4: NEW AMERICAN DRAMA/Akalaitis, Babe, Bosakowski, et al.

BEELZEBUB SONATA/Stanislaw I. Witkiewicz

DIVISION STREET AND OTHER PLAYS/Steve Tesich

TABLE SETTINGS/James Lapine

THE PRESIDENT AND EVE OF RETIREMENT/Thomas Bernhard

TWELVE DREAMS/James Lapine

COMEDY OF VANITY AND LIFE-TERMS/Elias Canetti

THE ENTHUSIASTS/Robert Musil

SICILIAN COMEDIES/Luigi Pirandello

RUSSIAN SATIRIC COMEDY/Babel, Bulgakov, et al.

GALLANT AND LIBERTINE/Marivaux, Beaumarchais, et al.

HAMLETMACHINE AND OTHER TEXTS FOR THE STAGE/Heiner Muller

MARGUERITE YOURCENAR: PLAYS

AN AMERICAN COMEDY & OTHER PLAYS/Richard Nelson

DOUBLES, DEMONS, AND DREAMERS: Collection of International Symbolist Drama

LAZZI: Routines of Commedia dell'Arte

DRAMACONTEMPORARY: CZECHOSLOVAKIA/Kundera, Havel, Kohout, et al.

DRAMACONTEMPORARY: SPAIN/Buero, Salom, Recuerda, Nieva, et al.

RAINER WERNER FASSBINDER: PLAYS

MARIA IRENE FORNES: PLAYS